THE
TALES
OF
INDIA

PART ONE

BY

DAULAT PANDAY

SRI AUROBINDO ASHRAM : INDIA

The Tales of India (Part One)

First Edition: 1969
Tenth Impression: 2005

Rs. 45.00
ISBN 81-7058-234-2

© Sri Aurobindo Ashram Trust 1969
Published by Sri Aurobindo Ashram Publication Department,
Pondicherry - 605 002
Website: http://sabda.sriaurobindoashram.org
Printed at Sri Aurobindo Ashram Press, Pondicherry
PRINTED IN INDIA

This book
is dedicated to the Divine Mother
of Sri Aurobindo Ashram, Pondicherry
with humble love and gratitude
from the author.

Contents

Contents

Prayers Have Wings

ONCE upon a time, two angels flew down from Heaven, to settle on the topmost branch of a tall pine tree in Kailas. It was a beautiful moonlight night, and all around among the snow-covered hills and valleys there reigned a silvery peace and silence. The angels looked around and saw that every now and then wings flapped in the still mountain air, and vanished Heavenwards.

"Who could these winged creatures be? And where could they be going?" Asked one angel of another.

"They are the prayers of human beings living on earth, and they are all flying upwards to reach the throne of the great God Brahman, the Creator of the Universe," replied the other.

"Have you noticed how pretty some of them are?" Asked the first angel.

"Yes, but most of them are quite ordinary, and a few seem to be positively ugly," replied the second. "Let us follow them and see where they are going." So saying they both spread their wings and flew up towards the fleecy clouds overhead. Higher and higher they flew, and as they soared upwards, they found that many of the winged creatures that were dark and ugly, could not go beyond the clouds, and fell back to earth and died. For these were the prayers of selfish greedy people who prayed for their own good, even at the cost of others. Other prayers, less ugly, but still not good enough to attain any height, pierced the clouds and melted in the rarer atmosphere above, like mist in the morning light. Whereas those sincere prayers that had come straight from the hearts of good and kind people, soared higher and higher, beyond the moon, and even beyond the farthest star.

When the angels had reached the gates of Heaven, they found a beautiful creature with translucent wings that shone like so many opals, waiting there. As they passed near it, they saw its face which was like an innocent child's, so frank and pure, that they could not doubt that it had come from a simple and honest heart.

The angels entered the gates of Heaven and passed into the hall where they found several beautiful creatures, but none to compare with the one they had just seen. They went together to the throne-room where they saw that these creatures conveyed their messages to the great God Brahman, and returned to the hearts that had sent them.

First came a pearly-winged prayer who bowed low and said, "Oh great Lord, I pray that there may be plenty in my land so that even the poorest may have enough." And to this the Lord Brahman replied "So may it be!" And the prayer backed away in silence whilst another took its place.

This one prayed for wisdom and courage, for it had come from the mighty heart of a warrior, and it too was soon granted.

Many others followed, but none of them were half as beautiful as the one the angels had seen at the gates. And just as they were wondering what had happened to it, the whole place was filled with a sweet fragrance, and soft strains of music commenced to fall upon their ears. The angels turned round to see from where these were coming, and lo! there stood the very one they had been thinking about. More lovely and opalescent than ever.

Bowing low before the throne of Brahman it said in a humble voice, "Oh Lord of all Creation, accept my deepest gratitude for the countless blessings that Thou hast bestowed upon me." Brahman was so pleased with this prayer that all Heaven overflowed with joy. The sun rose in all its glory, and rainbows danced in the heavenly skies.

"This prayer must have come from the heart of a King, or at least from a very wealthy man, for he could not be in want of anything. Otherwise he could not send up such a prayer," Said the second angel to the first. "Let us follow in its wake and see where it goes."

Thus both the angels followed it, and to their utmost surprise, they found that the beautiful creature led them to the hut of a poor beggar boy who was sleeping on the floor, and quickly entered his heart. Soon after this the boy woke up and smiled.

"I would like to test him and find out how he managed to send up such a prayer," said the first angel to the second. "So let us assume the shape of two weary travellers and go and speak to him." Thus they changed themselves into two travellers who looked very tired and hungry and knocked at the door. The little boy came out and received them with courtesy, and offered them all the fruits and nuts that he had collected after many days of toil. And when they expressed pity for his miserable condition, the boy only smiled and said, "I have much to be grateful for, kind sirs, for look at the sun which warms me the whole day long, and the birds that sing for me. There is also the music of rushing waters to soothe my ears, and the gentle winds to fan me to sleep. Even the King does not have more. And I am truly grateful for all these and so many more joys that the kind Lord has granted to me."

The angels looked at each other with surprise, and blessing the boy over and over again, they took their leave. Once they were out of his sight they changed their forms again and flew back to Heaven to tell this story.

King Janaka's Test

IN the reign of the great King Janaka, there lived a Yogi called Yajnavalkya, who was as much noted for his piety as for his wisdom.

Every morning while the golden dawn was slowly breaking over the far horizon, and the birds were singing their sweetest songs, Yajnavalkya bathed himself in the cool waters of a neighbouring stream and then went and sat on his dais to commence his discourse.

One morning he was preaching as usual to his disciples, among whom were learned Pandits, Sadhus (religious men), Sannyasins, (those who have renounced everything to take to the spiritual path), and many other men. These people noticed that Yajnavalkya their Guru, (Master or Teacher), was constantly looking at the door, as if he were expecting somebody. And they were not wrong. For Yajnavalkya was indeed waiting for his King, who also attended his discourses.

The disciples became jealous of this special attention given to the King. For, thought they, in the eyes of a spiritual man, a King or a commoner should be the same. So they could not understand why this special favour was given to Janaka. At last, they decided to ask their Guru why he was partial towards the King.

"Master," said one of them, "You are not quite fair to us if you place the King above us in your estimation. For, a man of God, like your worthy self, should not favour anybody in particular. Why then, do you have

A man came running into
the pavilion and shouted that the
king's palace was on fire.

a greater regard for Janaka. Is it simply because he happens to be our King?"

Yajnavalkya was surprised as well as pained at this question, which appeared quite ridiculous to him. "My brothers," said he, "You are greatly mistaken if you think that I prefer Janaka to any of you, just because he is a King. You will admit that we are all in duty bound to honour him as such. But Janaka is not only a King in the earthly sense of the word, but also in the spiritual sense. For he is a Siddha Purusha (a perfected man), and some day you shall see for yourself how true is this statement."

Some time after this incident, the great Yogi was once more preaching to his disciples in the presence of Janaka, when a man came running into the hut and shouted that the King's palace was on fire. He was wearing the uniform of the Royal Guard, and seemed greatly distressed.

No sooner had the news been delivered, than the whole place was thrown into utter confusion. Almost everybody got up and started to rush towards the palace. Some said that they had relatives working there, whereas others were afraid of missing the sight. Still others feared for the safety of their fields, which lay adjoining the palace grounds. King Janaka alone sat undisturbed, waiting for the confusion to subside, so that he could once again listen to the discourse of his Master.

The Guard who had brought the news was so astonished to see this, that fearing lest the King had not heard him right, again repeated the news, with greater emphasis.

The King was very annoyed at this, and answered, "You foolish man! Don't think that I have not heard what you have said. But do you imagine that I shall leave my place at the feet of my Master to go and save my earthly goods? Do you think I value them more than the golden words of wisdom I hear from my Master's lips? If my palace is on fire, let it burn! For such indeed must be the will of our Lord! If He wants it to be saved, there are better people than myself there, who will do their best."

Hearing these words even Yajnavalkya was surprised, and very pleased. He continued his preaching as if nothing had happened.

Some hours later, the disciples returned one by one, and you can imagine what a shock they must have got to see their King still sitting there. They recalled the words of their Master and felt ashamed of themselves, and bowed their heads at his feet. Never again did they doubt the wisdom of their Master. Is it any wonder then, that Janaka has always been remembered as one of the greatest Kings who ruled in those distant times!

The Blue Lotus

DEEP in the heart of the Himalayas, on the calm waters of a rippling lake, there once bloomed a blue lotus. So rare was her beauty, that the skies overhead blushed with pride, at sight of her, and the clouds hovered for hours over the mountain tops in sheer amazement.

But though the blue lotus was so beautiful, she was not at all proud, and opened her petals wide for the bees to collect the sweet honey she stored in her golden heart, and allowed the birds to alight on her stem and sing to her. Even the rabbits ventured to the edge of the lake to nibble at her great green leaves. And the wolf and bear confided their secrets to her.

Now, when she reached the marriageable age, her father the King of Lotus Land, sent his messengers far and wide to look for an equally handsome bridegroom for her. But though the eagles and falcons soared over the highest rocks and hills, and the Kingfisher dived into every mountain stream and lake, and the rabbits burrowed deeper and deeper into the earth, and all the animals searched in every possible and impossible place, they could not find another blue lotus to wed the Princess. So the poor Princess wept in silence, and implored her father to allow her to marry the Prince Pink Lotus, but her father would not consent to it.

At last Spring was over, and with the warm Summer months came a few botanists, in search of rare plants and flowers. And as soon as they saw the beautiful Princess, they forgot all about their hunger and fatigue, and at once made preparations to uproot and carry her away. The poor Princess turned quite pale and trembled in every petal.

She cried aloud for help, and because she was loved so well, the ladybear left her babies and hurried to her rescue, while the bees forgot their Queen and swarmed around the intruders. Even the birds and rabbits helped by eating away all the seeds and plants which the botanists had collected after many days of toil. So these poor men were compelled to retire in pain and confusion, to tell the world about the wonderful blue lotus they had seen blooming in the heart of the Himalayas, which story of course nobody believed.

The Princess Blue Lotus was saved, but the shock robbed her of her beautiful blue colour for good, and now she was only greenish-white, like so many of her sisters. But she was far happier, for nobody cared to carry her away as a rare flower, and her wedding day was at last fixed.

"Beauty has its price" the Blue Jay was heard to say to the Nightingale, "so it is safe not to possess too much of it."

The Rose and the Evening Star

ONCE a Sunbeam loved a Rose. But so did the Morning Dew and the Gentle Breeze. For the Rose, which grew at the edge of a forest lake, was fair with the creamy fairness of pearls, and pink, like the pale pink of sea-shells. But she did not care for any of these lovers. Her heart was given to the beautiful Evening Star that shone in the Heavens above.

In vain did the Sunbeam woo the Rose each day with his comforting warmth, and in vain did the Morning Dew cool her petals, or the Gentle Breeze sing his lullaby—

"Close your petals fairest lady,
For the sun is setting low,
All the flowers are getting ready,
To sleep and dream of the rainbow."

The Rose was only impatient, and scolded the Breeze thus "You silly Breeze, if you had the least bit of sense in you, you would not ask me to close my petals just when it is time for my Star to come. This is no time to sleep! I must look my very best, and smell my sweetest."

"But your Star is miles above you, how do you expect him to see you — let alone come down and meet you ?

"Only a stupid person like you could ask me such a question," replied the Rose. "Haven't you seen that he comes so often in the lake ? If you don't believe me, wait and you will soon see him in the calm waters below."

So the Gentle Breeze waited over the hill tops, till the sun had set, and the last bird had flown to its nest. And lo! just as the Rose had said, there was the Evening Star shining so beautifully in the waters.

The Rose saw him too and tried to appear more beautiful than ever by opening her petals wider. But this time she overstrained herself. And they broke off and fell softly on the waters of the lake and floated away.

"Oh, my petals! My beautiful pink and white petals!" cried the Rose. "Whatever shall I do without them ?" But the petals drifted further and further away, while the Evening Star shone as bright as ever in the Heavens, aloof and proud.

The poor Rose died, and the Gentle Breeze blew some dust over her, while the warm-hearted Sunbeam shone over her grave daily; and the Morning Dew shed his cool tears over her. But the Evening Star knew nothing of all this, and cared less.

Envy Brings Trouble

OUTSIDE a palace garden wall, there once grew a wild rose bush under a beautiful almond tree.

In summer when the dry winds blew over the plains and the poor bush was scorched with the heat, the almond tree bent low and gave it a protecting shade; and in Winter when both bush and tree were bare of every leaf and petal, the almond tree was a great comfort. For it helped to while away the cold lonely days with stories of things it had seen and heard, before the roses were born. Then Spring would come at last, tripping merrily over hill and dale, and both the tree and the bush would be once more in flower. The birds would return to sing in the blossoming branches, and the butterflies to kiss open each new bud.

It was just such a Springtime as this when the whole rose bush was in flower, and the bees hummed happily as they collected the honey, and the grass-hoppers skipped among the fresh green grass.

"How sweet is life and how happy we feel!" Said the roses dancing with delight.

"So do we", said the birds. "For we are full of song."

"But I am the happiest of all," said the almond tree, "For I am growing taller and taller every day, and soon I shall be able to spread my branches over the wall, and drop my blossoms in the palace garden."

"Oh, how fortunate you are!" said the rose bush. "I wish I were as tall as you, so that I could have a peep over the wall and see if there are any roses growing the other side."

"I shouldn't bother about that if I were you." said the woodpecker, who was busy pecking on a branch overhead.

"It's all very well for you to say that," said the roses in a chorus. "For you can fly over the wall and see everything, whereas we are stuck here and cannot move an inch."

"But so are we," said the buttercups. "And we don't mind it a bit. For after all we are not birds but flowers."

"All the same," said the roses turning towards the almond tree, "do let us know what lies beyond this wall as soon as you are tall enough to find out."

"Certainly, my dear," replied the almond tree. "And now let's forget about it and watch my blossoms waltz in the wind."

The days slipped away like happy dreams. Then one morning the almond tree suddenly shouted with joy, "Hurrah! I can at last look over the top of the wall."

"Oh, how wonderful," Said the rose bush excitedly. "Do tell me what you can see."

"There is a beautiful garden full of lovely flowers, and as for roses, why, I never dreamt that there could be so many in the world! But hush. Here comes the Prince with his friends."

"Oh, how we envy you!" Sighed the roses. "Is he very fair and handsome?"

"Yes he is as handsome and fair as any other prince of his kind. And he is holding a beautiful scarlet rose in his hand and stroking its petals."

"Oh dear, we almost feel like crying," sobbed the roses. "No prince ever comes to US."

"What does that matter? Don't WE come to you?" said the birds.

"Oh, YOU!" said the roses disdainfully. "How could you compare yourselves with a Prince of royal blood!"

"That may be true, but then WE love you, whereas he doesn't care a rap."

"YOUR love doesn't mean a thing to us." said the roses forgetting themselves. "We would have the Prince or nobody at all."

"Hush children. You shouldn't talk like that!" said the almond tree. "For it is very ungrateful".

"We don't care!" said the roses together. "In future please mind your own business, and stop preaching to us. And as for the rest of you." said they, turning towards the birds, "you can take your love elsewhere".

"Very well," said the birds sadly. And they all flew away one after another. The place was soon deserted, and the rose bush was left alone with her roses and her thoughts.

The almond tree was so offended, it turned its face away, and the rose bush lost the cool shelter of its friendly branches. And when summer came, the bush slowly withered and died.

Thus it was that envy brought trouble where all were so happy once. And the almond tree learnt the wisdom of silence.

Year after year came and went, and other flowers

took the place of the roses, but never a word did the almond tree say again as to what it saw behind that palace wall.

The Elephant's Revenge

THE elephant is said to be one of the most intelligent creatures in the animal kingdom. And this story will show you how well he can bear in mind any harm done to him.

A king once owned a white elephant of whom he was very fond. The Mahut (his caretaker) took him daily for a bath in the river, where several people gathered to pet and admire him. They brought bananas, bread and vegetables, and decorated him with garlands of bright flowers.

Now this elephant had to pass daily by a tailor's shop, on his way to the river. And the tailor's wife who was very fond of him, always kept some tit-bit ready for him.

One day it so happened that she was absent in the kitchen, when the beautiful animal arrived at her door, and her husband the tailor, who did not like the beast so much, and preferred to save the tasty morsels for himself, was seated near the steps. The elephant as usual extended his trunk to receive the gift, and the crafty tailor, taking this opportunity, picked up a long needle, and pricked the elephant's trunk hard with it.

The poor beast went away groaning with pain, and even the Mahut who had not seen the act, could not understand what was the matter.

Some weeks had passed after this incident, and the tailor went about his work as usual. The elephant

had stopped coming to his door, which pleased him very much.

Then came the great day of the King's birthday. The tailor was very busy preparing several new garments for the King and the court. On the day that they were almost ready, and only a few buttons remained to be tacked, the elephant who had been sent for his usual bath, suddenly appeared in the street. And a lot of people were cheering and dancing round him. But the tailor was too busy to notice all this, and his wife was away filling water at the well.

Nearer and nearer came the great white beast, and when he was only a few yards away, he threw a jet of dirty water straight into the tailor's face. This not only smeared his face with it but also spoilt most of the costly garments he was preparing.

It was the tailor's turn now to groan and swear, but he could do nothing, for the whole crowd cheered the elephant and enjoyed the joke.

Thus it was that the elephant took its revenge, for the tailor was dismissed from the court for having ruined the costly garments. And as long as he lived, he never forgot this bitter experience. And often repeated the story to all the children of the place, so that they may learn to respect this royal animal, and never play tricks upon him.

A Pearl of Great Price

FAR away in the depths of the Indian Ocean, there was once a beautiful island, which was well-known for its pearl-bearing oysters. The waters around this island were so clear, that the fishes who swam in them could see the palm fronds swaying overhead, or the great big ships laden with various merchandise, go sailing by.

Here on the sandy bed dwelt many oysters, big and small, who were often taken up by the divers for their pearls. The pearls were removed and they were either eaten by the islanders or thrown back into the ocean.

These oysters were rather jealous of one another, and never so happy, as when finding fault with their neighbours.

One night, when they had gathered as usual under the moonlit waters, to gossip and show off each other's treasures, a fat one came running to them, all excited and out of breath.

"Guess what I have seen today," she panted.

"A shark overhead," said one. But the fat one shook her head.

"A handsome Prince, in one of those steam ships," said another. But the fat one again shook her head.

"I know what," said a tiny one to her left.

"Then tell us quick", they all spoke together.

"You have seen a new star".

"NO" said the fat one. "You are nowhere near the

mark, so I might as well tell you what it is. I have seen a new arrival."

"A new arrival!" they said in a chorus. "Where is she? What is she like? Is she pretty? Has she got a pearl?"

"Now, now, not so fast!" scolded the fat one. "And for goodness' sake stop pulling and pushing me, or you won't hear anything." So they all stepped back and waited in silence.

"I was strolling past that big brown rock, when whom should I see but the ugliest, dirtiest oyster you can imagine. I wanted to find out more about her, but she was so ashamed of herself, that no sooner had she seen me approaching than she ran away behind the rock," said the fat one.

"Poor little thing!" said one of them who was not very pretty herself.

"Poor thing indeed!" said they in astonishment. "She has no business to be ugly. She will be a disgrace to our colony. I wish she would go and live elsewhere."

The next day however, they could not restrain their curiosity, so they all went in search of her behind the rocks and weeds. And there, to be sure, was a large oyster, greenish-brown in colour. Closer and closer they came, then one of them made bold to speak to her.

"How did you get here? And have you got a pearl to show?"

"I got here in the same way as all of you," said the new arrival shyly, "And I too have a pearl to show."

"Let's see it then. I hope it is better looking than yourself," said the fat one rudely.

"The new one cannot have a white pearl I am sure. For she is so dark herself," said another. And they all insisted on seeing the pearl, so the new one could do nothing better than show it to them.

"Look, how disgusting it is!" One of them screamed as soon as she had had a peep inside. And she turned her face away.

"Yes," said another. "It is almost black like herself."

"I had warned you. What did you expect?" sneered the fat one. The poor new comer was so hurt to hear this, that she quickly closed her shell and went away from there.

"How rude of you all to say such things!" said the one who was not pretty. "Supposing one of us had been in her place. How would we have enjoyed being told such things!"

"Since you are in such deep sympathy with her, why don't you too go and live with her?" said another oyster. "We are quite pretty and so we don't like to be in such company."

"Very well, if that is what you think, I will certainly be better off elsewhere," said the first, turning away.

Soon after this a terrible cyclone shook the island. The winds rushed like so many furies, and the waves dug up everything from the depths of the ocean and hurled it upon the shore. The new-comer too was dislodged from her place, and left on a rock, where a fisherman found her. He took her home and opening the shell he had a look inside. "What a strange kind of pearl this is!" said he to himself. "I must show it to the pearl merchant and see what he thinks about it."

And accordingly he hurried away to the merchant's house.

"What have you brought today my friend?" inquired the merchant.

"Please have a look at it yourself, for you will be the better judge," replied the fisherman handing over the oyster to the merchant.

The merchant opened the shell slowly and could not help exclaiming, "A BLACK PEARL! Where did you find it? It is a Beauty!"

The fisherman was so pleased to hear this that he made up a long story of how he had discovered the oyster high up on a rock. Then taking the gold pieces that the merchant gave him he hurried home to his wife to give the good news.

The pearl was passed from hand to hand, and the poor oyster had to pinch herself to find out that she was not dreaming. For after being looked upon with so much distaste by her fellow creatures, she could scarcely believe her ears when she heard all the praise that was lavished upon her. She was sent in a beautiful velvet case to the palace of no less a King than Akbar himself. And he had the pearl removed and fitted into his crown. And the oyster too was given an honoured place in his garden pond. And as long as he lived, the great Emperor never ceased to admire his find, and to praise it to his friends. "Which goes to prove," said one Angle Fish to another, on hearing this story, "that no one should be jugded by external appearances alone. For many a pearl of great price could lie hidden, behind a shabby covering."

Liroo-Lira

"LIROO, Lira," sang the nightingale in the jasmin bush. "Liroo, Lira," echoed the hills.

"Liroo, Lira?" asked the moon. "What is that?"

"Haven't you heard of Liroo and Lira?" said the nightingale.

"No indeed, I haven't, for as you see I am new," replied the moon.

"Oh! I see," said the nightingale." Then stop feeling shy and hiding your face behind your veils of cloud, and come down into the waters below. For I cannot sing so loudly."

So the moon came down into the hushed waters of the river nearby, the wind stopped whispering in the pine trees, and the crickets and cicadas too were silent. For when the nightingale sings everybody wants to listen.

"There was once a sweet little girl called Liroo," sang the nightingale. "Who loved her neighbour's son Lira, very dearly. Both the children had grown up together, and were never happy except when in each other's company."

"Their fathers were farmers whose fields lay side by side, and each helped the other to sow and to reap, to take the corn and the vegetables to the market, and come home laden with all kinds of nice things for their children."

"Now it was understood in both families that Liroo

was to marry Lira when she grew up, and the whole village looked forward to this event with joy. For there never was a better-looking pair in the world."

"But before the marriage day could be fixed, Yama, the God of Death happened to pass through their village, for he had been called to take away an old man there. And as soon as he saw the handsome Lira working in the fields, he decided to take him away too for his son-in-law."

"Oh dear! Poor little Lira!" sighed the moon. "What happened after that?"

"Don't interrupt me please," said the nightingale. "And you will hear everything."

"Now Yama's daughter too had reached the marriageable age," continued the nightingale, "and he had been told by his wife to keep his eyes open for a husband for her. So when he saw Lira, he decided that the boy would just be the right one, and made preparations to carry him away."

"So Lira fell ill that very night, and would have died. But when Yama came to take him away, Liroo wept bitterly and promised to give him anything in return, if only he would let Lira alone."

'Then give me your set of pearly-white teeth,' said Yama. 'For my daughter's have become yellow and disfigured. But do not mention this to anybody, or your Lira will die on the spot. If you do this I will let your boy live for another year.'

'Gladly,' said Liroo. And taking the whole set out of her mouth, she handed it over to him. 'For one year is a long time,' thought she. 'And we can get married in the meanwhile.'

"So Yama went away, and Lira recovered the next day to everybody's joy and surprise. But nobody knew of poor Liroo's sacrifice for the sake of the boy she loved."

"When Liroo went to bathe herself in the brook, and saw how ugly she looked without her teeth, she sat there and wept."

'How can I expect Lira to marry me now'? she moaned.

"Lira came running to her when he saw her crying," continued the nightingale, "And asked what was the matter. But she made no reply. For had she not promised Yama never to speak a word about it to anybody!"

"She only turned her face away and told her lover to look for another girl, because she had become too ugly for him. Lira was so shocked to hear this, specially as he did not understand the reason, and pleaded with her to tell him what was the matter. He took her gently into his arms and assured her that she was as lovely as ever, and he loved her very much. Then slowly Liroo lifted her face and showed him her toothless mouth."

"How terrible!" said the cicadas. And they started chirping together.

"Once again I ask you all to keep quiet," said the nightingale angrily. "Or this story will never be finished." So the cicadas swallowed their chirps and everybody said "Sh..." together. And all was silent once again.

"Lira was horrified to see his beloved's mouth empty

of all teeth," sang the nightingale. "And thinking that
some evil witch had taken them away from her, he
caressed her cheek and said that it did not matter to him
at all whether she had a single tooth in her mouth or
not. To him at least, she would ever be the same dear
old girl that he loved."

"What a sweet boy!" whispered the wind in the
pine trees.

"Sh..." said everybody together. So the wind fell
silent. And the nightingale continued.

"Days passed by, but now Lira's parents seeing
that Liroo had somehow lost all her teeth and was not
able to eat her food as usual, or to go about her work in
the same happy way, decided that after all she may not
be the most suitable bride for her son. And they set
about finding another girl."

"How mean of them!" murmured the brook. But
the nightingale took no notice. She was getting used to
such interruptions by now.

"But Lira swore that he would never marry another
girl", continued she. "So they had to leave matters
at that."

"Hear! hear!" said all her audience together. They
had entered into the spirit of the story, and there was no
stopping them.

"The year soon passed," sang the nightingale, "and
once again Yama came knocking at the door to carry
away the boy. And once again Liroo wept and pleaded
with him, and promised to give him anything he wanted
if only he would go away and leave her lover alone."

'Then give me your hair' said Yama. 'For my

daughter's has become quite faded, and she will be glad to have yours.'

'Gladly,' said Liroo. 'And let the God of Death take it all away.'

"So Lira was allowed to live. But Liroo became the Ugliest girl in the village. And when she saw herself in the waters of the brook, she screamed and ran away into the woods. In vain did Lira and the whole village search for her, they could not find her anywhere."

"The boy who was now deprived of his beloved, went half mad with grief and despair. He refused to take his food and became so thin that his parents were sure that he would die. They sent their friends to distant towns and villages to bring the prettiest girls for him to choose. But he turned away in disgust from them, and would not even look their way."

"That's the way of a true love!" sighed the moon. "I wonder if I will ever be able to find somebody to love me as truly!"

"Why not?" said the water-lily who had just opened his petals, and was already in love with the new moon. "If you will consider my suit, I will be honoured to become your husband".

"Now if you have finished with choosing husbands for yourselves, I can get on with my story," Said the nightingale.

"By all means," said they together. "For we are anxious to learn what happened after that".

"The year was over once again," said the nightingale, and Yama came to take the boy away. There was no Liroo now to save him. So away he took the boy in his

black chariot drawn by four splendid black horses.
Down, down, they went. Right into the heart of the
earth, where Yama had his palace of black marble.
And a thousand of his citizens came to receive him."

"Among them were also his wife and daughter, you
can be sure," said the nightingale. "But when the daughter saw what a thin scarecrow of a man her father had
brought for her, instead of a handsome youth, that he
had promised, she was very angry indeed."

'Is this your idea of a handsome man?' she asked
Yama. 'Have you no consideration for my feelings?'

'He was not like this when I first saw him,' explained
her father. 'But owing to the separation from his
beloved girl Liroo who gladly gave her teeth and hair
so that he may live two more years, he has become like
this!'

'You were a fool not to have carried him away at the
time instead of listening to the silly girl's pleas said the
wife. 'So now you may take him back again to his na-
tive place, for I could never stand the sight of such a
son-in-law in my house.'

'And take these too with you,' said the daughter
throwing the teeth and hair that her father had brought
for her, after him. 'They do not fit me in any case.
And I look much better without them'

"That's wonderful!" said the crickets together.
'Now tell us the end quickly, for it will soon be daylight
and you will stop singing."

"All right then keep quiet for goodness' sake," said
the nightingale "and listen."

"So Yama took the poor boy back to his village and

threw the teeth and hair too on top of him and went away. Lira who had seen and felt all this as if in a dream, woke up with a start. 'Where could I have been?' He asked himself. 'If it was only a dream, where did these my beloved Liroo's hair and teeth come from?' He ran out to the woods shouting her name and asking her to come back to him, for he knew the whole story now. And he had also brought back her teeth and hair."

"The sparrows who heard him carried the message to the heart of the wood where Liroo was hiding, and begged of her to return to him. And return she did, straight into his arms."

"Hurray!' shouted everybody together. And hugged each other with joy. The Water-Lily hugged the moon, and told her that it was good that she had no hair or teeth, otherwise what would he have done if they had been taken away?'

"What happened after that?" demanded the wind, who was tired of waiting in the pine trees.

"Why, Lira gave back the teeth and hair to his beloved, and she was as lovely as ever. They were soon married after that, and lived happily ever after."

"Just as we two shall also do very soon," Said the water-lily taking the young moon into his arms. "Won't we?"

"If you wish", whispered the moon shyly.

And everybody present wished them all joy.

Karim's Story

IT was the custom in the village of Moondi to gather in front of an open fire in the cold winter evenings and while away the time in telling stories. And this is the story that Karim the grocer's son told the company.

Once upon a time, two men were taking a walk on the seashore, when they found an oyster and began to quarrel about it. "I saw it first", said one man. "And so it belongs to me."

"But I picked it up," said the other. "And so I have a right to keep it."

As they were quarrelling thus, a lawyer happened to pass that way, and both of them decided to let him settle the dispute.

"Learned sir," said the first man. "We were both walking upon this seashore just a few minutes ago, when I saw this oyster. But my friend happened to be quicker than I, and so he picked it up, and now he refuses to give it to me. Won't you please try to convince him that it belongs to me?"

"I will not give it up," said the second man. "I picked it up, and so I have a right to keep it."

Now the lawyer was a clever man, as lawyers usually are, and so he soon found a way to settle the dispute. But first he said to them, "You will have to accept my decision no matter what it may be. Otherwise you may take your case elsewhere."

"By all means, we will accept your decision," said

both the men together.

"It seems that you both have a claim to this oyster, so I will divide it equally between you two," continued the lawyer. "And you will then be completely satisfied."

No sooner had he uttered these words, than he opened the oyster, and before either of the men could say anything, he swallowed its contents. And very gravely handed to each man one empty shell.

"But you have eaten the oyster," said the first man.

"Ah", said the lawyer. "That was my fee for deciding the case. But I divided what remained in a fair and just manner."

You can be sure that the two men were quite crestfallen on seeing this, but there was nothing that they could now do about it. It taught them a lesson never to quarrel again. And each of them went his way.

Abdulla and the Little Brown Bottle

ABDULLA owned a junk shop at the junction of the two roads in Jalalabad. There were bottles and boxes and vases of all kinds, and odds and ends of many things, which the people of the town had rejected from their homes from time to time.

An old table whose marble top had long been sold, but which still served a purpose, having been fixed with two planks on the top, and a chair with one leg missing, but which could also be used by propping it against the wall, were the only furniture there. And Abdulla had reserved them for those of his clients whom he could not possibly expect to be seated on the mat on the floor.

Day after day, people brought all kinds of things to be sold, but few came to buy anything. So Abdulla became poorer and poorer while the junk overflowed on to the footpath.

One day, in the month of April, when the heat was so great, that people walked close to the walls, hugging the scanty shade that they gave, Abdulla was seated on his doorstep fanning himself with a piece of cardboard, when an old man came to him with a little brown bottle in his hand. He looked more like a beggar than anything else, for his clothes were dirty and torn, his hair unkempt, and the stubble on his chin gave him a fierce appearance.

"How much will you give me for this little bottle?" he asked Abdulla handing the bottle over to him.

Abdulla took the bottle, turned it over in the palm of his hand, and returned it to the beggar in haste saying, "I am afraid it is not worth anything my friend, and I have dozens of them here which nobody wants to buy." Then he saw that the poor beggar was very much hurt at these words, and being a kind-hearted man, he pulled out the only Rupee note that he had, and gave it to the man saying, "Here is something that may help you for a while, and may Allah help you after that."

The beggar gratefully accepted the money and went away, pressing the little bottle into Abdulla's hands.

Soon after, Abdulla's wife Fatima brought his lunch, and remembering the poor beggar who had just left, Abdulla ran into the street to call him back to share it with him. But though he looked everywhere and asked all his neighbours, there was no trace of him. People whom Abdulla asked about the beggar, thought the heat had affected the poor junkman, and advised him to keep to his shop instead of looking for somebody who had never passed that way.

Abdulla was annoyed at this, for he knew that he had not been dreaming. He had the little brown bottle in his hand to prove that such a man had actually been there. At last he gave up the search and went and took his scanty meal.

Then, after his wife had departed, he sat on his

door step again, and examined the bottle carefully. There was a red label on it on which was written the following :

"Fill me with water, shake and take,
     For old or new disease' sake.
But tell no soul of this my charm,
     For that will only do you harm."

Abdulla laughed aloud saying, "If all diseases were cured so easily, there wouldn't be a sick man left in the world."

He was still laughing when a poor lame boy came to purchase an empty tin of kerosene from him. Abdulla thought that this was a good chance to try the charm of the bottle, so he said to the boy, "I will give you your tin for half the price if you will drink a little water for me." The boy was surprised at this strange request, but the thought of saving half the money for something else was very pleasing, so he readily accepted.

Abdulla went into the shop, and following the directions carefully returned with the water in the cup, and gave it to the boy, who swallowed it in one gulp.

"If your leg feels better tomorrow," said Abdulla, "come and drink some more of it".

The boy went away feeling very happy indeed, and Abdulla too was smiling, for he felt amused at the thought of this strange deed.

Next day Abdulla opened his shop very early, and waited impatiently for the boy to return. For he was

She worried him daily
to confide his secret to her.

curious to know if the so-called charm of the bottle had actually worked. But it was nearly noon before he saw somebody like him approaching the shop, together with an old woman carrying a child in her arms.

"May Allah bless you a thousand times, sir, for, curing my poor son," "said the woman. And since you are such a wonderful Hakim (doctor), I have brought this my youngest too to you. For she is suffering from constant attacks of fever."

Abdulla asked the woman to be seated, and then going inside, prepared the water as before and gave it to her. The woman made her sick child drink it, and then went her way, blessing Abdulla several times. The boy thanked Abdulla over and over again, and jumped with joy for having recovered the use of his legs.

The story of this miracle spread very quickly, and each day more and more people thronged to the junk shop. Rich people threw money and jewels at Abdulla's feet, so now he was rich enough to put himself up in a proper dispensary, which he did very soon.

His wife, however, was not content with this change of fortune, and nagged him daily to ask for more and more money for his cures. She was also very curious to know how Abdulla managed to cure all these people with only a few spoonfuls of water. And in spite of his protests, she worried him daily to confide his secret to her.

At last when she found that she would never succeed

in getting it out of him, she played a trick on him. She told him that she would be away for a day, visiting her brother who had called her, and then keeping the back door unlocked, she went out of the front door wishing him goodbye. Then she returned through a lane to the back door, and opening it just a little, watched Abdulla at his work. Then when he was busy with his patients in the front, she quietly slipped inside, examined the bottle, and replaced it after reading the label.

Since that very moment, the bottle lost its magic powers, and poor Abdulla was puzzled to find that it no longer cured anybody.

Those who had blessed him once began to curse him now. And even accuse him of robbing them. Though he never asked for a pie from anybody.

Finally he was hauled before a Magistrate for practising Black Magic and ruining people's lives and was thrown into prison awaiting trial.

In vain did the poor man plead his innocence. Nobody believed him.

When his case came to court, all the evidence was against him, and he was about to be sentenced to a long term of imprisonment, when an old beggar stepped out from among the crowd, and begged the Magistrate to grant him a few minutes.

He assured the court that Abdulla was completely innocent, and to prove it, he asked for the little brown bottle to be given to him.

He whispered a few magical words into the bottle and then handed it back to Abdulla, asking him to proceed as usual with it.

An old blind man was brought from the streets, and Abdulla was given a cup, and some water too.

Abdulla turned away from his audience and then did the usual thing of filling the bottle with the water, giving it a good shake, and handing the water to the blind man to drink.

Lo! the miracle took place once again, to the utter astonishment of the whole court.

Abdulla was set free among loud cheers from everybody present, and as he was going out, the old beggar approached him. Abdulla thanked him profusely for saving his life. But the old beggar smiled at him, and asked him to hand over the little brown bottle to him, for now that everybody knew its secret, it would never be able to work in the same way again.

Then he turned angrily to Fatima and said "As for you, woman, if you had not played that nasty trick upon your poor husband, you would have lived like a Princess for the rest of your life. And Abdulla would have left his name in medical history. Let this teach you to respect his wishes hereafter."

Abdulla went back to sell his junk a sadder and wiser man, and the people of Jalalabad always spoke of him with love and respect.

Good Luck for Sale

WHERE the seven roads met in a town in Bihar, there once came a traveller with his servant, and pitched his tent in the shade of a pipal tree. The next day he put up a board on which was written "Good Luck for Sale. Buy it for a Rupee, and be happy."

The inhabitants of the town were naturally very surprised to read this. For they had heard of vegetables for sale, and also of fruits and grains, and houses and fields, and everything else under the sun, but never in all their long lives, nor in the lives of their fathers, had they ever heard of good luck being sold. So they shook their heads suspiciously and swore to their neighbours that they would never be deceived by such a man.

But who can resist the temptation of trying his luck? Specially if it is only for one Rupee! So the same people, when their neighbours were busy elsewhere, sneaked off quietly and entered the tent.

The pedlar treated them with great respect and after taking their money, directed each along a different road, or to a different house, where his supposed "Good Luck" was waiting for him.

Of course, all this was false. And the only good luck that ever happened to be there was with the pedlar himself. For he alone was taking the people's money, and getting rich all the time.

So the people were very angry, and decided to teach him a lesson. One of them dressed up as a Nawab and went to the pedlar in his tent. And the pedlar treated him with still greater respect, and offered to help him find his good luck.

The Nawab said that by the grace of God he had already found it long ago, and was living in great comfort. But seeing how much good work the pedlar was doing, for the poor people of the town, he had come to invite him to his home, where he was giving a feast in his honour.

The pedlar was so overwhelmed with this, that he accepted the invitation with pleasure. And set off with his assistant to the Nawab's dwelling, which was not very far away.

The so-called Nawab led his guests to the terrace of his house and ordered his servants to bring water to wash the feet of both his guests. And scarcely had the servants done so, when there was a cry from the streets below, of fire.

"Fire! Fire"! shouted the people and ran as fast as they could.

"Where is the fire?" asked the Nawab.

And the servants leaned over the wall of the terrace and said "It seems to be somewhere near the tent of our honoured guests."

"What?" shouted both the guests together and ran to the wall and leaned over to verify. And indeed it was just where the servants had feared.

"Oh, it is my tent which is on fire! What shall we do now?" said the pedlar hitting his head against the wall. "All my good luck was inside it".

Seeing the great distress of his guests the Nawab

ordered his servants to run and help the people to put
out the fire as soon as possible. Then turning to the
pedlar and placing a hand on his shoulder he said "Do
not worry about your good luck my friend. It is only
going up in a vapour to Heaven to wait for you there.
You will surely find it as easily as the rest of these
people who came to you for help. So let us proceed
with the feast for I am hungry." So saying he led his
guests inside. But both the guests had lost their appe-
tite, and could not eat a thing. The pedlar understood
the trick that had been played upon him, but what
could he say? Had he not deserved it after fooling so
many people? So silently he got up and went away
attended by his helper.

The Two Sisters

THERE was once a very wealthy villager who had married twice and had two daughters, one by each wife.

Sudha, the daughter of his first wife was dark in complexion, and plain looking. Yet she was loved by everybody for she had a sweet disposition, whereas Suniti, the daughter of his second wife was not so popular, in spite of being pretty, for she did not care for anybody but herself.

As the girls grew up, Suniti constantly quarrelled with her sister, and one day matters became so bad that poor Sudha left her home and went and sat in an adjoining field and cried and cried as if her heart were about to break. A rabbit who heard her, came out of its burrow and asked her what was the cause of her grief. Sudha told him everything and he was filled with pity for her. "Dry your tears little girl and come with me to the kingdom of the Underground. The Princess who reigns there is very kind, and if you will try to please her, she will allow you to take away with you something which will change the whole of your life."

Sudha thanked the rabbit very much and then catching hold of his little tail they entered his burrow and went on and on till they came to an iron gate which was locked. The rabbit knocked thrice upon it, and it was opened by the keeper who seemed to know the rabbit, for he bowed low and said "You are most welcome to the city of the Underground."

Sudha said goodbye to the kind rabbit who did not wish to accompany her, but who promised to be at the same gate when she returned, and then went inside. To her surprise she found herself in the grounds of the palace where the sun shone brightly, and flowers of all colours danced merrily in the breeze. She was so much taken up by the beauty of the scene that she forgot her troubles and felt very happy. The Princess came out to greet her as if she already knew of her coming, and asked the girl if she would like to do a little work for her.

"Certainly, Your Highness," replied Sudha. "I will do anything you wish to be done."

"Then please look after my cows, hens, and cats, because I cannot find anybody who loves them enough."

Sudha was delighted to be entrusted with this work for she loved all animals, and was ever eager to help them. If this was all that the Princess wanted her to do, it would be fun, she thought. And she ran to the cowshed and patted the white-and-brown cows saying "You must be hungry my beauties, I will fetch you some hay and clean water. Then I shall spread some straw on the floor for you to lie upon."

"Thank you little girl," lowed the cows. They were so pleased with her that they gave her much more milk than they were giving to any other servant of the royal household. Then when she had finished milking them and made them comfortable, about half a dozen cats tripped in and started purring and rubbing their backs against Sudha's sari. "We are very thirsty so won't you please give us some milk?"

"My poor little pussies, of course you will have your milk", said Sudha, and she fetched their basin and filled it up with the fresh milk, which the cats soon lapped up and then curled up and went to sleep.

Next Sudha went to the store-room to see about the corn and all the fowls came running after her crying "We too want our corn, so please don't forget us."

"You poor little darlings," said Suddha scattering a good handful on the floor. The fowls finished the corn eagerly and then flapped their wings in thanks. They gave Sudha many more eggs to take to the Princess, who was so pleased with her that she wanted her to stay in the palace for good. But Sudha who was afraid of her step-mother, thanked the Princess kindly, and begged to be allowed to return home, for if she was found missing, she would get a good scolding.

"In that case I must not detain you any more." said the Princess. "But I would like you to take home a present from me by way of reward for what you have done. So go up to my room and you will find several boxes on a table. Choose and bring to me the one you like best."

So Sudha went up to the room and just as the Princess had told her, she found several boxes on a beautiful table inlaid with mother-of-pearl. There were boxes made of jade and ivory; also of coral, sandlewood and marble. And all of them were covered with precious stones which twinkled like so many eyes at her. She was sure that these boxes contained jewels that she had no right to take away from the Princess, even if she was asked to do so. Besides what had she done for her, except look after her pets for a day? So she chose a plain wooden box which was hidden under the others and did not look very pretty either. Then she went down and gave it to the Princess who was very surprised at her choice. "I wonder what made you choose this box when there were so many others far more beautiful?" said the Princess.

Sudha assured her that she was more than pleased with her choice and after thanking Her Royal Highness and taking leave of her pets, she returned to the gate. The rabbit was waiting for her as he had promised to do, and once more she caught hold of his tail and they both came up to the same spot near her house. She thanked him from the bottom of her heart and then ran home as fast as she could. Her step-mother who was busy making chapatties did not even look at her as she entered timidly, but her sister saw the box in her hands and at once grabbed it saying "From where did you get this?" Sudha told her all that had passed and Suniti hastily opened the box and slipped on to her finger the beautiful diamond ring which she found inside. Her mother too came over to have a look at it and she was very pleased for once.

No sooner had Suniti worn the ring than a great change seemed to take place in her. All the hardness and selfishness in her heart melted away as if by magic, and she hugged her sister affectionately saying, "My dear sister, how very kind of you to give me this wonderful gift! But I cannot accept it for it really belongs to you, and nothing will give me greater pleasure than seeing you wear it." So saying she handed the ring back to Sudha whose joy knew no bounds for the change it had brought in her sister. The two of them became friends ever after, and lived in peace and happiness.

The Turquoise Blue Rose

MADHUPUSHPA was the daughter of a King and as lovely as the dawn, which broke like the opening of a golden rose each morning. She had no brothers and sisters and the King, her father, was so fond of her, that he could not bear to let her out of his sight. So the young Princess followed her father wherever he went, and learnt all the arts that he practised. She could ride a horse and draw a bow as skilfully as any of her father's archers, and with greater grace.

One day she was out hunting as usual when her horse shied suddenly, reared on his hind legs, and then galloped off in a different direction, as if he had seen a tiger. In vain did the Princess try to stop him. He galloped all the faster, and would have plunged with her into a deep ravine, had not a woodcutter's son stopped him at the risk of his own life.

"You have saved my life, " said the Princess to him when she had recovered from the shock. "So ask anything that you desire, and I shall see that my father gives it to you."

"Fair lady," said Ramakaran, the woodcutter's son, "I am only a poor man who earns his living by cutting wood and carting it to the city to sell. How could I dare to ask for anything from so beautiful and highborn a lady as yourself!"

"Do not be afraid of speaking your mind, O woodcutter," said the Princess. "For if I had died, my

parents would have lost their only child, and this kingdom its Princess."

It was then that Ramkaran realised that the beautiful
lady before him was the Princess he had heard so much
about, and not a nobleman's daughter, as he had imagined. He fell at her feet and said, "Noble lady, all that
this your humble slave desires is to serve you. So
command, and I shall lay down my very life for you."

The Princess felt so happy at hearing this, that she
took him with her to her father's palace. There she told
her fond parent all that had befallen her, and begged him
to allow her to keep this brave man as her bodyguard.
And this the King readily agreed to do.

Days passed and became months, and being in each
other's company every day, Madhupushpa and Ramkaran grew to love one another more and more. And to
rely on each other for help and advice. At last a time
came when Ramkaran could no more hide his love for
the Princess, and with her permission, made bold to
speak to the King her father about it, and ask for her
hand in marriage.

The King was so enraged to hear this, that he had
Ramkaran flogged and thrown into prison.

When the Princess heard of this, her sorrow knew no
bounds, and she refused to touch food or drink till he
was restored to her.

As you can very well imagine, this was far from what
her father desired, but what could he do? If his only
child were to die, the world would come to an end for
him. So he had to give in. But he did so with a heavy
heart. It was then that the Queen had a brilliant idea.

"We will send him to fetch us a turquoise blue rose," said she. "And to return within a year, or give up his life."

"A turquoise blue rose"! exclaimed the King. "I have never heard of it. If such a flower exists, how is it that my gardener has never tried to grow it in our palace gardens? He knows very well how fond I am of roses!"

"Calm yourself my worthy Lord," said the Queen. "There certainly is NO such flower in the world. That is the very reason why we shall ask him to bring it. Set him to do the impossible, and he will either perish in the attempt, or come to us empty handed. Then we can do what we like with him. The Princess is sure to forget him, once he is out of her sight, and when the year is over, we shall marry her to a more worthy person."

The King was delighted at this idea, and calling Ramakaran to him, he told him under what conditions he could marry his daughter. And added, "You are well aware how fond I am of roses, so if you succeed in getting me a plant on which blooms this marvellous rose, I shall be most delighted. And I will not only give you my daughter in marriage, but make you King in my stead, and retire to the forest to spend the rest of my days in prayers and meditation."

When the Princess heard this, she was very sad indeed, for she was sure her beloved would never be able to find such a flower, and die on the way. So she took a vow that if he did not return to her by next Summer, she would leave her father's palace and go in search of him.

Ramakaran however, was full of hope, and told her to be of good cheer. And to pray for him daily. As his love was pure and true, he felt sure that he would return to her bearing the plant that her father desired. He set out the very next day, and Madhupushpa no longer went hunting with her father, but spent all her time in prayers for her young lover.

After leaving the city walls, Ramakaran came to a deep forest into which he plunged with zest and looked at every flowering tree and bush for the blue rose. But never found anything like it anywhere. And all the people he asked, only laughed at him, and took him to be crazy.

After several days of wandering, he came to the other end of the forest and found a tall mountain range stretching endlessly before him. "Perhaps the rose grows in these mountains," said he to himself. And commenced to search once again. He had already become so weak with hunger and fatigue that he found it difficult to move quickly, but he paid no attention to it, and went on searching everywhere.

He looked where the brook went murmuring past, and where the waterfalls thundered in cascades. He looked where the winds played catch-can on the hill tops, and where the moonbeams lingered over the sleeping buds. He also looked where the birds nested among the tall trees, and where the sunlight played hide-and-seek over rock and pebble, but there was no sign of the turquoise blue rose. And people of whom he asked only fooled him, and laughed behind his back.

Some told him to go south to Cape Comorin, and

then cross over to Lanka, (Ceylon), for he was sure to
find it blooming in the King's garden at Anuradhapu-
ram while others directed him to look for it at the
foot of the rainbow, among the pearl strewn waters of
the Maladive islands. But Ramakaran was too dejected
to follow all this. He thought of his Madhupushpa
miles away from him and wept bitterly. For he was sure
now that he would never be able to marry her. As his
tears fell on the rock and washed away the dirt which
had been there, he saw a strange vein of blue colour in
the rock on which he was sitting. He looked at it for a
long while and then scraped away the mud to see what
the colour was like. And lo! it was a beautiful blue.
"If these rocks are blue in some parts, I wonder if there
are any blue flowers growing nearby that are also of the
same colour," said he to himself. And he looked everywhere along the rocks and soon found what he was
seeking. For now that the earth was vibrating under his
feet with the promise of Spring, there were plenty of
wild flowers everywhere, and some of them were a
beautiful turquoise blue. But what he wanted was a
rose, and there were no roses in these parts. So he
searched all along the way, and at last came upon a wild
rose plant growing high up on a hill. He carefully dug
it out, and carrying it to the blue rocks, he transplanted
it there. Then he waited from day to day, to see if the
roses that were a common white, would take on a bluish
colour. And after a month or so of careful work, the rose
bush started giving truly blue flowers. At sight of them
he fell on his knees and offered a prayer of thanks to
God who had at last guided him to the right place.

When Ramakaran was quite sure that the roses were now of the desired shade of blue, he once again dug the whole bush out of the ground and placed it in a basket. Then he started on his long journey home.

The way was indeed very long, and every now and then he had to stop and go in search of water, or to wait till the sun was less strong. But after many days of patient travel, he saw the minarets of his favourite City, and was outside the gate the same day.

News had somehow travelled before him, about his return with the Rose plant, and the whole city had turned out to welcome him.

The King himself had been informed, and there he was on his bejewelled elephant, waiting to receive him. He had been sorry for having sent away his daughter's young lover in this way, for he could no longer induce her to take part in anything now, and the news of his return had filled him with joy. Besides, he was very anxious to know how his future son-in-law had succeeded in finding something which did not exist.

Nearer and nearer came Ramakaran, carrying the basket of roses on his head, and placed them at the feet of the elephant, who carefully picked it up with its trunk, and handed the gift to the King on his back. And the King was so dumbfounded at the sight of the perfect turquoise blue roses that he could not even speak for joy.

A great feast was held in honour of the occasion, and preparations were set afoot for the celebration of the marriage of the Princess. And throughout the land there was rejoicing.

The Princess was perfectly happy now, and after the wedding was over, the King handed over the charge of his kingdom to his children, and retired to the forest to spend the rest of his days in prayers and meditation, just as he had promised. And the kingdom became rich and prospered a great deal, for Ramakaran had unknowingly discovered a turquoise mine in the mountains, and rich merchants from all over the world came to buy these gems. Besides, to this day, it has remained the only place where bloom these marvellous roses, and people come from far and near to gaze in wonder at their beauty and unique colour.

Dotty Goes to Poona

DOTTY was a poor mongrel who had just missed being an April fool by being born on the second of April. Till he was nearly a month old, his mother could not decide what to call him, because he was not like any other puppy whom you could call Moti, or Snooty, or Fido, or Leo. He was a funny sort of fellow who was always getting into other people's way, or running in the wrong direction. And nobody could guess what he would do next.

One evening an old friend of his mother happened to call, and no sooner had she spied him than she exclaimed "What a funny little kid you have got there! Excuse me if I seem a bit rude, but this boy of yours seems to be a bit dotty."

"I am afraid you are not far wrong," said the poor mother. But she added in his defence, "It is not really his fault. For he takes after his father who was not quite right in the head, if you know what I mean."

"Oh yes, I understand," said the friend sympathetically. "I dare say he will grow out of it." And no sooner had the stranger gone, than all his brothers and sisters started teasing him. "He is dotty! He is dotty!" And so the name stuck to him.

But Dotty was a sporting fellow and did not mind being called Dotty, and later made up for all his shortcomings by learning to bark, yelp, howl and growl, much before the others. And so they were compelled to respect him.

As he grew up, Dotty also learnt to hunt for rats, who ran in and out of the wooden boxes and other junk which was lying under the counter of the teastall where he was born. His brothers and sisters helped him in this, and what fun it was to fall over each other when the chase was hot! Or to be the first to grab any bit of bread, or other tit-bit, that happened to tumble on to the floor, from the tables in the stall. And as for noise, that too was part of the fun. For this teastall was on a railway station, and every few minutes a train rolled in with a lot of clatter, and went out screaming. But what was most fascinating to the puppies, and most mysterious too, were the moving forest of legs that hurried past them. But like all good things, this fun too soon came to an end one day.

Dotty was asleep behind a Coca-Cola box, whilst the others were playing with the chappals of the stall owner, which unfortunately, he had removed from his feet, to sit more comfortably on his high stool. And what with one of the puppies pulling one way, and two others trying desperately to snatch it away, the straps were soon torn asunder. Then the toe pieces were chewed up, as if they had been chicken chops. So when the stall owner tried to retrieve his property all he found under his foot was a very wet and unshapely mess. And he was very annoyed. He did not know that like human children, teething puppies too have a craving for chewing things, and should be given something to bite.

The stall keeper sent for the railway policeman, and

ordered him to take the puppies far away, and leave
them there. But how far away they were taken, Dotty
was never to know, and his mother only turned her face
away in sorrow, whenever he happened to mention the
subject. So he had to drop it, though he felt very lonely
and missed his brothers and sisters a lot. He cried and
slept, and when he woke up he cried again. But what
was the use? Nobody heard him. And nobody cared.

He too would have suffered the same fate, but soon
after this his mother took him away to another place a
little further on, and for a few days she remained with
him almost all the time. She told him all the little doggy
tales she knew, and brought to him many little things to
play with, from the platform.

Life was just beginning to be pleasant again, when a
strange-looking black dog came and smelt his mother
all over, and whispered something into her ear. She
got up and followed him, and Dotty was about to do the
same, when he got so entangled in a lady's sari, that
she had to help him out and place him safely in a
corner. But no sooner had she commenced to walk,
and the sari to swish, than with a jump, he was after her
again. "You naughty little fellow," said the lady, who
was more amused than annoyed by his antics. Then
once again she lifted him and took him to a safe place.
But Dotty being what he was, took this to be as good a
game as any, and was just about to follow her, when he
got locked up in what seemed to him a forest of moving
legs, from which he had to be rescued by a kind-hearted
shoe-shine called Babu.

Babu had always loved dogs, and was delighted with

Dotty, so he took him to his place and tied him with a rope to stop him from wandering and getting into people's way. But if there is anything a dog hates, it is being tied up. So he wriggled and twisted, and tugged and chewed at the rope, till at last he was free once again. And before Babu could catch him, he was once again lost among the moving legs of people on the platform.

When he came out of it once again he was delighted to find his mother. But that strange black dog was also with her, so she ignored him, and even growled when he approached her. He was very hungry, and did not know what to do about his dinner, so he just sat down in the middle of the vast place near the ticket office and whimpered. Fortunately for him, Babu who had been looking for him all over the place, found him. And poor little Dotty was so glad, for he was feeling quite lost and lonely.

Babu took him home to a very small room under a staircase, and gave him a little bread and milk. There were three little children too in the room, who never seemed to tire of caressing him. And he felt so happy, that he licked their hands and feet in gratitude.

Life had become interesting once again, and even when a collar was slipped round his neck, to which a long chain was attached, he did not mind it much, because his master loved him, and was always playing with him.

Everyday he accompanied Babu to the station, and sat or slept near him while his master worked. And many a time Babu's customers brought a biscuit or a piece of bread for him, and stopped to fondle him.

Days passed very quickly and became weeks, and weeks became months. Dotty had forgotten the past and grown into quite a good-mannered dog, when the very worst happened. His master was suddenly taken ill and died in a few days. Of course, Dotty like many other dogs, had felt beforehand that some such thing was in the offing. So he had never left his master's side, even when the chain had been removed, and he had been allowed to roam where he liked. And now that his master was no more, he was so heart-broken, that he refused to eat or drink for several days. And daily he went to the station and sat by himself at the place where his master was accustomed to work, hoping that by some miracle he would return to the place.

At last, after many days of waiting and fasting, while he was roaming about on one of the platforms, he saw a beautiful little dog sitting on top of a suitcase. He approached cautiously, and tried to sniff her at a distance. For he knew that besides being a lady-dog, this stranger was something quite different from any other type he had so far seen. And just as he was about to draw a little nearer, the lady-dog said in a very refined voice.

"Please don't come any nearer."

"Why not?" asked Dotty surprised.

"Because I have got a pedigree," she said.

"What's a pedigree?" asked Dotty. For he had never heard such a word.

"It is something very special and tells you who your

grandfather was, and so on," replied the lady-dog.

"Is that all?" asked Dotty.

"No, that is not all. But I don't think you would understand if I were to tell you. Besides, I am in a hurry. For we are going to Poona by the next train to attend the Dog Show, and my master will be here any moment," said the lady-dog.

Dotty was just about to ask where was Poona, and many other questions, such as why she wore her hair so long, when all the dogs he had seen so far had only short hair. But her master came striding along and took her away saying "Come along Lizzy, or we will miss the train." And poor Dotty was left standing where he was.

He roamed about here and there searching for food, and finally came to another part of the station, where he saw a horse being led into a wagon. After he was put inside, the wagon was not closed immediately, so Dotty slipped in when the keeper was busy arranging the hay and other things for his comfort. Then with a big bang the door was closed and bolted. And for what seemed ages, the train never moved. But he was so tired and sleepy that he did not care. All that mattered to him now was to go to Poona. And he was sure that all trains that went puffing and whistling out of the station must be going there.

Many hours later, the train stopped. And the doors were opened. Dotty stretched himself, and got out first. For he felt very much cramped and did not care much for the smell of hay.

"Hello!" said a gruff old man with a big moustache.

"Look what has come out of the wagon. I ordered a horse, and they send me a dog along with him."

"Isn't he sweet?" said a small girl who was standing near him.

"Please daddy, do let me keep him."

"But you can have a much better dog any day, my pet. He looks very grubby and he is only a mongrel," said the gruff old man.

"Oh daddy, don't say such things. I am sure he understands, and it will hurt his feelings," pleaded the little girl, bending down and stroking the head of the poor dog.

Dotty was so happy to find somebody who cared for him that he not only wagged his tail for all he was worth, but also licked her hands and gave his right paw to shake, as his late master had taught him to do. This went in his favour, and the gruff old man smiled. And while he was busy with the horse, the little girl led him to their station wagon outside, to wait for her father.

That is how Dotty arrived at Poona. Or so at least he thought. For in reality it was not Poona at all but quite a different place. But what did it matter? He had found a good home and kind masters with whom he remained to the end of his days. And he was perfectly happy and content.

Katch-Kan the Naughty Crow

ONCE upon a time, a family of crows lived high up on a Neem tree in a garden. They had many neighbours, and they were all busy at the same work—house-building.

Mr and Mrs Kaw, as the family called themselves, had four children, and the youngest was the laziest and most mischievous of them all. His name was Katch-Kan, and you would be surprised at the tricks he could be up to. If his father said "just help me a bit to collect some twigs for our nest", he would only flick his tail, or flap his wings, and fly away to another tree.

One day Katch-Kan saw that their neighbours the Long-Beaks were mending their last season's nest on the mango tree. So when they were not looking, he crept up cautiously and pulled out one twig and carried it away in his beak. The Long-Beaks did not notice it at the time so he did it again.

Now Mrs Long-Beak was a busy crow, and when she saw that her nest was not getting any bigger than what it was when she started, she was annoyed. "We are not getting on, can't you work any faster?" she snapped at her husband. "I am doing my best," mumbled Mr Long-Beak. Just then their daughter Goo-Goo who had gone to find some bread crumbs for their breakfast, returned.

"Please help me to finish our nest first dear," whispered her father, "or your mother will be very angry." So Goo-Goo put away the bread crumbs in a hole in the tree, and quickly flew away to fetch some twigs. To her surprise, she found another crow flying in the same direction behind her. So she sat down on one of the branches of a tall tree, and watched if the other crow would do the same. But the other crow who was our naughty Katch-Kan, flew past her, carrying a twig in his beak. And then he dropped it a few steps away, where there was already a small heap of them. This made Goo-Goo very curious, so quickly picking up the same twig, she followed this crow to see what he was upto.

She found that the crow she had followed sat on the branch on which was her parent's nest, pretending to preen himself. Then when her parents were busy with something else, he quickly pulled out another twig from the nest and flew away with it. She understood now why her poor father was not able to get on with his nest. So next time when Katch-Kan pulled out another twig, she swooped upon him and shouted "Thief! Thief!"

She told her parents what she had seen, and Mr and Mrs Long-Beak naturally carried the complaint to Mr Kaw about his son, and soon the whole colony knew about Katch-Kan.

"You aught to be ashamed of yourself!" said Mr Kaw. "Stealing your neighbour's twigs!" But Katch-Kan only flicked his tail and flew away chuckling.

At last they decided to ask Red-Beak the parrot for advice, for he was known to be very clever, and knew the whole alphabet, and could even recite it backwards.

"I know what you should do," said Mr Red-Beak after listening patiently to Mr Kaw. "You should engage two sparrows to spy on your son, and whenever he does a thing like this they must put him to shame by telling everybody about it." So two sparrows the Misses Chitter and Chatter were engaged to follow Katch-Kan about, and see that he behaved himself. But even this did not help to change him, so Mr Wise the owl advised the colony to appoint Katch-Kan as night watchman. "For," said Mr Wise, "if he is kept awake all night, he will be so sleepy during the day, that he will not be able to do any mischief."

So Katch-Kan was made night watchman from that very day. But what do you think the naughty crow did? He started calling them at all hours of the night, shouting at the top of his voice, "wake up! wake up! you sleepy heads! or you will be roasted alive! For I see a fire below."

You can imagine how panicky the whole colony must have been to hear this in the middle of the night. They all woke up and started squawking and flying helter skelter, dashing against each other, and against the trunks of trees. But Katch-Kan was very pleased with himself, and laughed so much that many of his feathers fell off.

Next morning however, several crows came and pecked at him, and they would have killed him, but the kind-hearted Goo-Goo told them to leave him to her, and she promised to change him. So Katch-Kan was left in her charge, and the first thing she did was to make him go and collect all the twigs that he had pulled out from the parent's nest. She made a nice new nest out of it, and lined it with cottonwool which too Katch-Kan had to fetch from very far away. The cry was always for more twigs and more wool, so Katch-Kan had no time to think about any mischief.

When the nest was ready, Goo-Goo laid four bluish-green eggs in it, and Katch-Kan was quite delighted with them, and could scarcely wait to see them hatch.

In a few days his labour was rewarded, and four little crowlets came out of them. And now it was: "More food! More food!" The whole day long. And Katch-Kan had a very busy time stuffing their beaks, but he was so happy and proud of them, that he forgot all about his mischievous ways, and became a changed crow after that. And when the family grew up, he made himself useful to all of them and made them such comfortable nests, that the whole colony was proud of him.

The Gardener and the Pumpkin

ONCE upon a time there was a poor gardener by the name of Manu who worked for a rich merchant in a town. He swept the garden, weeded the lawns and watered every tree and shrub that grew there.

One day, as he was digging a trench at the foot of a mango tree, he looked up and saw a number of parrots pecking at the ripening fruits. "Kai kai, krr, chuck kai..." said one parrot to another. "Here are plenty of nice juicy fruits."

Hearing this, all the other parrots came and perched upon the same tree, and Manu had a lot of difficulty driving them away.

"I wonder why a small fruit like a mango is made to grow on a tall and strong tree like this one, while a huge pumpkin is grown on a delicate creeper! Now if I had the power to change these things, I would grow the pumpkin on a fine strong tree, and the mangoes on a bush," said he to himself.

As he was musing thus, another gardener who worked as his assistant came along and asked what he was muttering to himself.

"I was just wondering," said Manu, "why God hangs so light a fruit as a mango on so tall and solid a tree, while he allows a big pumpkin to grow on a delicate

creeper?"

"There must be a good reason for it," answered the assistant, "which we are too ignorant to understand."

"To me it seems a foolish thing. That's all," said Manu. "Look at all the trouble I have in chasing away the birds that keep pecking at the fruits constantly. Besides, how much easier it would be for me to pluck the fruits if God had grown them at a convenient height. For year after year I have to climb to the topmost branch at the risk of my life to collect these mangoes."

As they were talking thus, the maid-servant came out to say that the mistress desired some fresh flowers for her "puja" (worship), and so the gardeners hurried away to pluck them.

Many days passed away, and the gardener Manu was working under the same mango tree once again when a big fruit dropped upon his head with a thud.

"Help!" Shouted Manu. "I have broken my head... I feel quite faint..."

Hearing him cry out thus, his assistant came running and poured some water over his head. Manu was not much hurt, except that there was a small bump on his head where the fruit had hit him.

"If you make so much fuss about a mango, what would you have done if a nice big pumpkin had fallen on your head?" asked his assistant.

"Yes, thank God it was only a mango," said Manu. "Otherwise my head would have cracked like a coconut shell. How foolish I was to think that it would have been much better to grow the pumpkin on a tall and strong tree!"

Frinu the Fish

IN the centre of a Sultan's palace garden, there was a very large and lovely pool. It had a tiled border of mango-green and the deep gold of ripe coconuts, and on its surface floated a number of lotuses, like clouds on tree tops, on a dew-wet morning.

In this pool lived a few fishes, who were the favourites of the little Prince, who looked after them personally, and fed them with all kinds of choice sea-foods. The result was, that these fishes had become so fat and lazy, that they could scarcely wave their fins or shake their tails, and lay all day drowsing in the shadow of the lotus leaves.

One day, just as they had finished their sumptuous meal, which the Prince himself had brought for them, they heard a lot of noise outside the grating, and rushed there to see what was the matter. To their surprise, they saw a whole shoal of the most wonderful scarlet and gold fishes, pushing each other, and laughing and joking among themselves.

"Look at those fat creatures, how ugly they look!" said one of them pointing a delicate fin.

"They are so clumsy, that when they try to turn round, they just fall over each other. Not in all the wide ocean have I seen anything so funny," said another, laughing till she trembled all over.

"Oh do let me have a peep at them," said a third who had just come, and who was so pretty that the poor fishes in the pool could scarcely dare to look at her.

"Yes indeed!" said she backing away in haste. "They are simply frightful! Why on earth do they eat so much? If I had been in their place I would rather have starved and died, than look like them!" And she gathered her gauzy fins like two rainbowed scarves round her, and glided away laughing.

One by one the others too slid away, and for some minutes after, their tinkling laughter, like so many pearl-bells set in motion, echoed among the weeds outside.

The fat fishes in the pool however, took little notice of them, for they were so greedy that they could not afford to give up eating, just because a bunch of pretty maids had laughed at them. "They are jealous of us," said the fattest. "That is why they made all those rude remarks. I am sure that not one of them could have tasted the things we eat everyday..."

But among these fishes in the pool, there was a young boy-fish called Frinu, who was not of the same opinion, and felt very hurt and unhappy. For he had fallen in love with the lovely little maid, who had found them so ugly. And he determined to starve himself till he became slim and graceful like her. So from that day onwards, when the Prince brought them their meal, he hid under the lotus leaves, or spent his time doing one exercise after another, or in dreaming of his beloved with the rainbowed fins, whose name was Fri.

Thus everyday, he lost a little of his weight, and though he spent hours before the grating in the hope of seeing her once again, she never returned. And her tinkling laughter haunted him all the time. He never gave up his fast. For he intended to become so slim, that he would be able to swim past the grating, and go in search of her.

The day came at last, when with a mighty effort and the loss of several scales, he managed to squeeze himself out. And though it hurt him, he was happy. For he was free, and soon he would find his loved one and show her how slender he had become.

He swam down the water channels, until he got to the river, and then down the river, until he came to the sea.

The sea was like a looking-glass and merged into the sky with hardly a dividing line. And the sun shimmered through the mist like a lantern seen through a dull glass.

Among the coral groves, he met shoals of brilliantly coloured angel fish, with their scales of silverblue and yellow. And the red fire fish, and the multi-coloured peacock fish. But there was no sign of Fri. And fishes he consulted, told him to look for her among the coral castles and weed forests of the ocean.

At last, on the tenth day of his escape, he found his loved one. And she was lovelier than ever. And when she waved her gauzy fins about her, he was so bewitched, that he could not even wish her a good morning. At the same moment she too spied him, and calling her friends around her, she said, "Look at that poor miserable fellow over there. Did you ever see a more sickly looking fish? Why even his scales have fallen off, and he looks positively ugly." And once again she laughed her tinkling laughter like so many pearl-bells set in motion, and sailed away, leaving poor Frinu to gaze after her.

You can imagine what Frinu must have felt. He was so broken-hearted and faint with hunger and disappointment, that he hid in a dark cavern near-by, and lay himself down to die. "She called me ugly when I was fat, and now that I have undergone such trouble and become thin for her sake, she still finds me ugly!" said he to himself. And he hid himself in the darkness and closed his eyes in despair.

He did not know how long he had lain there, and whether it was day or night. But when at last he opened his eyes, he found himself in a beautiful room of pink and mother-of-pearl. Soft sea-shell music fell on his ears, and a lovely large rock-rose lay besides him on the pillow, to soothe and fill his moments with its perfume. As he looked around him, he saw a beautiful maiden-fish with stars all over the body, and fins of moonlight, sitting near his tail.

"Are you feeling better now, fair sir?" She asked softly. Frinu was so astonished to hear this, that he felt sure he was dreaming, and at any moment he would wake up, and find himself alone with his misery.

He gazed for a long moment at her and then asked, "Who are you, gracious lady? and where am I?"

The fair maid whose name was Shihiri (the starry one) then spoke and said, "I ought to explain to you everything to dispel your confusion. But I am afraid you are still weak, so please drink a little of this wine first. It is made from sea-cherries from my father's garden, and after you feel stronger we shall talk about everything." So Frinu drank the wine gratefully, and then listened to Shihiri's story.

"When I was born," said she, "one of our court astrologers said that when I came of age, my parents must look in the cavern adjoining the palace, and they would find there a young male fish who would be my future husband. Accordingly, my parents had given orders to all our courtiers to watch the cavern daily, and to report to them what they saw. And the day before yesterday, one of them reported to my father, the great King Zuk, of these southern seas, that they had found a young male-fish lying in the deeps of the cavern. My father hurried there with our physician, and had you brought here. For you were more dead than alive. And he ordered me to wait on you personally. He will be very pleased to hear that you have at last recovered, for then he can give orders to prepare for our marriage."

Frinu could scarcely believe his ears, and he tried to protest against what he thought to be a grave mistake. But the sweet Princess Shihiri would not listen to him. He told her all about himself, and how he had loved the lovely little Fri.

Shihiri was shocked to learn how badly he had been treated by her. "If you will consent to be my husband." said she shyly, "I will do my best to make up for the ill treatment you have received at her hands." So Frinu could not do better than give his consent, and the marriage was celebrated with great pomp.

Every fish for miles around was invited to take part in the rejoicing, and many a star fell into the ocean on that day, to twinkle among the amber sands.

Just when the ceremony was over, and everybody was congratulating the young couple, who should come forward but pretty little Fri, waving her rainbowed scarf-like fins about her. But when she saw Frinu with his lovely bride, she almost fainted with fright and jealousy. For she felt sure that Frinu was a Prince after all, and she had missed the opportunity of being his bride.

So out of spite, she spat on the nelwy-wedded Princess, and everybody fell upon her and would have killed her; but Shihiri pushed them aside and tried to calm her down. Fri had lost all her pretty scarlet and gold colour in the fight, and her fins too were torn from her body. But Shihiri was too well-bred to rejoice in the plight of her rival, and ordered her maids to fetch her a new pair of fins that were purple and gold. And to dye her body a wonderful sunflower yellow. This made her once again a very charming creature, and she was so overcome with remorse that she begged their forgiveness and departed hastily. And Shihiri and Frinu were left alone to enjoy their happiness in peace.

Unity Is Strength

IN the village of Methi Pala there once lived a very poor man with his family. Not finding any work for himself and the others, he decided to go elsewhere and try his luck. So he ordered his wife to make everything ready for their departure, and set out the very next day.

They travelled many miles on foot, resting under the shades of trees, and eating what little they had brought with them.

On the fifth day of their outing, all the food and water that they had brought with them was exhausted. So the old man asked his family to stop under a big Pipal tree, because there was a stream of water not very far away, and it seemed a suitable place.

He ordered his daughter to sweep the ground under the tree. To his daughter-in-law he gave the task of filling all the empty pots with fresh water, and sent his son to collect wood for the fire. He told his grandson to make a stove ready with stones and bricks for cooking the evening meal. His wife was also given some work. She had to take all the cooking pots and pans to the stream and after scrubbing them well, keep them ready for cooking. The old man himself was not idle either. He set out to see what he could collect for their meal.

After searching here and there, he happened to see a monkey on top of the very tree under which they had decided to rest. The monkey also had been watching all that was going on below, and being curious by nature, came down to find out what all the noise was about. He said to the old man, "You don't seem to have a grain of food with you, so what are you making all this fuss about?"

The old man answered "My dear friend, YOU will provide the very food that I have been searching for this past many hours, so prepare to die. We will be able to feast on you till we can find something else."

The monkey was terrified to hear this. He had noticed how everyone in the family had worked in harmony since their arrival, and obeyed the orders of the old man. So he felt sure that they would unitedly kill him, and there was no hope of his escape.

He approached the old man and said, "My good sir, you may feed upon me as you have decided to do, but after all how long is my flesh to last? Will you let me go if I give you the means to live comfortably for many years to come?"

The old man thought over this and then replied, "If it is truly as you say I will not take your life."

The monkey was delighted to hear this and at once climbed the tree and fetched a bag full of gold coins, and laid it at the old man's feet. You can be sure that the latter was overjoyed with this unexpected present, and ordered his whole family to pack up, for they were returning home.

He showed the coins to all the members of his family, who hugged each other and danced for joy. They hastened to the nearest village and bought some food

and other things for themselves. Then they hired a
bullock cart and returned home.

The neighbours were very surprised to see the family
come back and settle in their old home once again.
They asked all sorts of questions, and when they had
learnt everything they too decided to try their luck in
the same place. Accordingly they made all preparations
and set out the very next day. Arriving under the very
same tree, they set to work at once. The head of the
family ordered his wife to make a big fire, but the wife
answered, "Let us first of all find the monkey, if he is
not here what will be the use of a fire?"

When the daughter of the house was told to go and
fetch some water from the stream, she turned away and
said, "Why should I go? The path is full of thorns.
Why don't you ask my brother to do it?" And when
the son was told to fetch some wood for the fire, he
replied, "Where is the necessity of bringing wood,
when what we want is a bag of gold from the monkey?"

The monkey who was seated on a branch overhead,
heard all this, and decided that this family could not
possibly succeed in harming him, because there was no
unity among them. So when the head of the family
came and told him to prepare for death, he only laughed
and asked him to go away.

The head-man was very surprised to hear this, and
he called upon all the members of the family to help
him to kill the monkey. But they all answered that it
was not their business to do so. The poor old man who
badly needed the bag of gold, started to climb the tree
alone in the hope of catching the monkey. But the

monkey was too agile for him and even threw stones and other things at him. He was forced to come down once again, and the whole family had to return home empty-handed, because there was no unity among them.

Riches of the Heart

ONCE upon a time there was a great famine in Gujerat. Hundreds of people lost their lives. Among them were Ramesh's parents, so the little boy had to go and live with his uncle in Surat, and help him to carry parcels from the railway station, in his wheel-barrow.

Sometimes they had only a short distance to go, and then they were paid very little. On other days when they pushed and heaved over the long winding streets, and across the bridge, they had earned enough for a glass of whey, or a cup of tea and a few *jelabies*.

Ramesh was quite happy with his uncle. But one day a motor lorry suddenly rushed upon them and knocked them over. The wheel-barrow was completely broken and all the parcels damaged. Ramesh's uncle died on the spot, but Ramesh himself was removed to the hospital, where he recovered after several months.

Now the poor boy was all alone in the world and as he was afraid of the Police, who constantly put all sorts of questions to him about the accident he ran away to Navsari, and began his life all over again as a beggar.

Day after day, he sat on the main street where lots of rich people passed, while the hot sun beat upon him mercilessly. And he got weaker and weaker from hunger and loneliness.

One day Ramesh saw a rich man getting out of his car near a shop. So mustering all his courage he approached him saying, "Please sir, give me a paisa, for

I am very hungry."

"Why should I give you a paisa?" said the rich man. "Haven't you got hands and feet to earn it?"

"Alas sir," sighed Ramesh. "I have my hands and feet, and would gladly earn my living if I could find a job. So won't you kindly help me?"

"Get out of my way, and let me pass," said the rich man rudely. "Do you think that I have nothing else to do than to waste my time trying to find work for vaga-bonds like you?"

Although this was not the first time that Ramesh had received a rebuff, it brought tears to his eyes, and he went and sat dejectedly in a corner.

Towards evening that same day, a lame old man who walked with the help of a crutch, and whose dirty clothes were patched in several places, passed that way. As he came near the boy he bent down awkwardly and said in a low voice, "Take these my son. I have had enough for today, and there is plenty left over." And he emptied the contents of his pocket in Ramesh's lap.

Ramesh looked down and found that there was half a chapatty, a two anna piece, a partly soiled tomato, and a few pieces of bread, in his lap.

"But you must keep these for tomorrow," said Ramesh, who was feeling ashamed to take away all these from the poor man. For he knew how difficult it was to collect them.

"No my son," said the old man, patting the boy's head with his horny fingers. "God will take care of tomorrow, as He has taken care of today. In the mean-time eat this and make a poor man happy."

Ramesh was so touched with these words that he could not help saying, "So many rich people passed this way, and they had not a paisa to spare for me. And you my poor friend, who are even worse off than myself, come and give me all you have."

"That is all right, my son," said the old man. "For there are many kinds of riches in this world. And poor people like you and I are only blessed with the riches of the heart."

The Witch of Kamalalaya

THE village of Kamala-
laya which nestles at
the foot of the lower Himalayas, is indeed a very pretty
place. Surrounded by tall trees, and having a tiny lake
near by, which is covered by pink and white lotuses in
the summer, you would think it was a corner of Heaven
itself. It is from this little lake that the village took its
name, for Kamalalaya means the abode of lotuses.

In this village there once dwelt a shrivelled old woman
who was called a witch by the ignorant and superstitious
people of the place. Not because she had any magical
powers, but because she was cleverer than the rest, and
used her common sense more than they.

Now in this village were many shepherds who took
their sheep to graze on the surrounding hills. Among
them was a shepherd boy called Kirmin, who loved his
flock of sheep dearly.

Every morning, before the smoke-like mist had scarcely lifted off the lotuses, Kirmin could be seen along
the narrow lane leading up the mountain, driving his
sheep before him.

At last, when he came to an open place which was
covered with thick grass, and dotted with wild flowers
he sat down among the fragrant pine needles, and commenced to play his flute. This was a sign for the sheep
to stop there and graze. And a happier flock you could
scarcely have seen, for they frolicked and gambolled all
over the place.

Some hours later, when they had eaten all they could of the lush grass, Kirmin took them to a nearby brook for a drink. Here they nudged and pushed each other with their horns to reach the cool clear water, and kneeling on their front feet drank thirstily.

When they had finished, he counted them, and if the number was correct he tapped his stick three times on a rock, which was a signal for them to take the homeward path. But sometimes it happened that one or two strayed elsewhere, then Kirmin would have to go in search of them, and when they had once more been gathered into the flock, he would drive them home again.

On this particular day however, one of the week-old lambs, was missing, and search for it as he may, he could not find it, or hear it bleat anywhere. So with a heavy heart he drove the rest of them back to his village. Then he told about the missing lamb to his comrades, and five of the village boys offered to help him look for it. So back they went to the same place, and spread out in different directions.

At last one of the boys spotted the lamb high up on a rocky slope, eating some of those wild yellow flowers that sheep love so much, but which grow between rocks on the mountains. He called out to the other boys, and they came running, delighted to have found the little one after all.

But though they called and shouted, played their flutes and tapped their sticks, the lamb paid no heed, and went on plucking at the flowers, as if nothing else mattered in the world.

Kirmin was in tears by now, for he loved all the

members of his flock dearly, and he knew that if the lamb was not rescued before nightfall, it would either be eaten by the wild animals roaming these parts, or die of cold up there. He beseeched his friends to find some way, but they shook their heads sadly, and said that he would have to leave the lamb to its fate.

Then one of them remembered the old woman who was a witch, and who lived not too far from the place. "Go to her," said he. "I am afraid she is your only hope. If she is a real witch, she will use her magic to bring the lamb back to you."

"That's a good idea," said Kirmin. "Let's all go together." "No fears!" said they in a chorus. "It is YOUR lamb, so you must go alone."

"She might turn me into a stone" said one of them.

"Yes," said another. "Or she might even make a meal of us all, if we went." And one by one they crept away leaving poor Kirmin to his fate.

Kirmin looked up at the lamb, all alone there, bleating helplessly, now that it had finished its meal, and decided to risk everything to save it.

He ran as quickly as his legs could carry him, and knocked at the witch's hut. As there was no answer, he pushed open the door and went in and there on a torn mat was an old woman fast asleep. Kirmin shook her gently saying, "Mother witch, mother witch, please get up".

The witch opened her eyes and got up with a start. She was angry with the boy for having called her a witch. But seeing how frightened and sad he looked, she smiled at him and said quietly, "What is the matter, my son?"

Kirmin hastily told her what had happened, and begged of her to use her magic to rescue the lamb for him. On hearing this, the old woman laughed. But it was not an unpleasant laugh, so Kirmin lost his fear of her. Then wrapping a torn wollen shawl over her shoulders, and taking her stout stick, a rope, and three pieces of cloth with her, she told the boy to lead the way.

In a short time they arrived at the foot of the huge rock, and after looking everywhere carefully the old woman said, "It is surely not from here that this poor creature has been able to climb up, but from some other place. So let us first look for it." So saying they both commenced to look everywhere.

After a long while they came upon a tiny path, which though dangerous, seemed the only one by means of which the lamb could have scaled up the height. And the old woman told Kirmin to follow the path, and find out where it led.

Kirmin readily did as he was told, for he was anxious to rescue his lamb. And when he had gone right up to the place from which he could see the lamb, the old woman shouted to him to return by the same way, and this he did.

"Take these my son," said the old woman when he was down once again. She handed him the rope and the three pieces of cloth, saying, "when you have once more reached the top, lie on your stomach, and gently ease yourself forward, till you can slip the noose in the rope over the head of the lamb. Then return to the top backwards, and never even once look down in the valley.

Keep your eyes fixed on the lamb. When you are safe and away from the edge, pull the lamb up, who though protesting, will come. Quickly tie this cloth over the eyes, and with these two other pieces, bind its feet. Use the rope to fasten her to your back, and descend slowly, with your mind fixed on one step only at a time. When you are coming down, hold on to the grass and bushes that are firmly rooted among the rocks, and do not pay attention to the bleating of the lamb. You are a courageous boy, and I am sure that if you do as I say, we shall soon be safely on our way home."

Kirmin smiled, and then taking the rope and the three pieces of cloth with him, he carefully commenced to scale the height once again. But the next thing to do was not easy. However, he found plenty of those sweet yellow flowers at one place, so plucking them, and offering them to the lamb, he enticed and dragged the frightened animal out of danger. Then while it was eating the flowers he bound its legs, and blindfolded it with those strips of cloth. He swung it over his shoulders and tied it firmly to his body, with the rope.

Now the most difficult part began. But he kept repeating to himself what the old woman had told him, and ignoring the lamb's bleatings, and keeping his mind fixed on taking only one step at a time, he was down safely, sooner than he had thought.

"Shabash! My son," said the old woman when he was once again with her. "You are indeed a hero! Now I will see you safely to your village and then hasten home." So the boy took the lamb in his arms, after removing the rope and strips of cloths, and they took the homeward path.

Night had already fallen, and the villagers were fast asleep when they reached there. Only Kirmin's poor mother was sitting up, weeping for her son, whom she was sure had come to harm through the old witch. Imagine her surprise and joy, when her son returned to her, hale and hearty, carrying the lamb in his arms.

As for the old woman, she had slipped away quietly as soon as she was sure that the boy was safe. He told his story to his mother, and assured her that the old woman was no witch, but a very clever lady, whom it was a shame to treat in this manner.

The next day the whole village knew the story. And when Kirmin went to return the rope and pieces of cloth, almost the whole village went with him. And they were so ashamed of themselves that they joined the palms of their hands together, and begged for her forgiveness and blessings. Then they implored her to come and live with them and be their mother and guide. This the old woman readily agreed to do, because she too was rather lonely. And many were the happy years she spent among them before she died. She helped much to drive away their superstitions and to enlighten them and also taught them to use their brains and common sense, and not to be led away by silly fears of the supernatural.

The Princess
was so beautiful
she put the moon
to shame.

Kanji's Dog

ONCE upon a time a poor old man lay dying, so he called his eldest son to him and asked him what he would advise him to do about the few things he possessed in this world, before he passed away.

The son whose name was Kanji, and who was a very considerate boy, said, "Dear father, may you live with us for many a golden year yet, but if God desires your presence elsewhere, I would like you to leave this hut to our mother, who on becoming a widow at your passing away, will not be able to fend for herself. And give away the patch of land you own, to my younger brother, who is too young to do anything else, except till the soil."

"And what about you dear son"? asked the father. "Don't you want something for yourself?"

"Do not worry about me, dear father," said Kanji. "For all I want from you is your blessings. I am old and strong enough to look after myself. And I hope soon to be able to make my way in the world."

The father was very pleased to hear this, and placing his hand upon Kanji's head, he blessed him several times. Then he took an old purse from under his pillow, and gave it to his son saying, "Keep this as a token of remembrance from me. May it never be empty of what you need. But do not fall into the temptation of misusing its powers for selfish ends." Kanji thanked his father for everything, and the old man fell into a happy sleep from which he never awoke.

A few months later, Kanji took leave of his mother and brother, and set out with her blessings, taking the purse that his father had given him. His mother made him some chapatties and chutney and Kanji felt as happy as a bird, and as light of heart.

For many days he trod along the road which he had taken, hoping to reach a town and find some work there. But there was no sign of it as yet. At last he decided to take some rest, and was about to finish the last of the food that his mother had given him, when he saw a miserable little mongrel coming towards him. Now

Kanji was a kind-hearted boy, so he gave away his food
to the dog, and also fetched some water for him in a
coconut shell. The dog was very grateful for this, and
coming up to his new master he licked his feet and
thanked him. He also let the boy know by his looks,
that hereafter he would never leave him. Kanji too was
glad of his newly found friend, and both the boy and
the dog stretched themselves under a tree and were
soon fast asleep.

They could scarcely have slept for an hour, when
they were rudely awakened by three men who wanted
to rob the boy of everything. But the dog though weak
fell upon them with such fury, that they were soon
frightened away. Kanji was very pleased with the
little animal, and carried him along with him, when
next day he once again took to the road.

At last they reached a large town where the boy found
that everybody was enjoying a holiday, and drums and
pipes were being played at every street corner. So he
asked an old man what was the cause of all the rejoicing.
"Don't you know that today our dear princess Tara
holds her Swayumvar ?" Which means the ceremony of
choosing a husband.

"No indeed", replied Kanji. "I am a stranger who
has just arrived to this place in search of work. So how
should I know?"

"If you want work," said the old man, "you had
better ask at the palace gate, for I am sure that there
will be plenty to do inside. Many a handsome Prince
has arrived there, so you will not be turned away."
Kanji thanked the old man and made for the palace

gate with his dog.

"What are you doing here with that dirty dog of yours?" asked the palace guard, as soon as he saw Kanji approaching.

"I am looking for some work in the palace; for, I was told that there would be plenty to do there today," replied Kanji.

"Sure there will be plenty of work for you, but first you must drive away that beastly companion of yours," said the guard.

"NEVER!" said Kanji angrily. "He and I will never part company as long as we live."

"Then go your way, for I cannot allow you to pass through this gate." So saying the guard pushed poor Kanji aside rudely, and closed the gate.

Now it so happened that the Princess had been at her trellised window having a peep at the Princes below. And she saw and heard everything that had passed at her gate. She sent her maid to tell the guard to open the gate and let the boy in. Then she came on her balcony thinking that she would not be seen from there, and instructed her gardener to give the boy some work. "If he can care so much for a mere dog," said she to one of her hand-maidens, "he must be a good boy." And she secretly decided to choose him for her husband.

Now Kanji, who had been waiting below, saw the Princess and fell in love with her at once. He had no mind to do any work now, for all he desired was to get himself dressed as a Prince, and compete for her hand. Accordingly he went in a corner, and taking out the purse from his pocket he started shaking it again and again. For he had learnt by now that each time he shook it, a couple of Rupees fell out of it. At last when a heap of money had been collected, Kanji left the work and set off to the market to buy himself a horse and some princely garments. The poor dog tried its best to restrain him by placing his paw upon his master's hand, when he saw the latter misusing the power of the purse, but Kanji pushed him aside and told him to mind his own business. And to stay away from him.

The little animal was so sad at being thus cast aside, that he did not know where to go. He decided to wait for his master's return outside the gate.

Kanji came back to the palace in the evening, and now that he was dressed as a Prince, the guard admitted him with much bowing of his head, and told the other servants to make him comfortable in the palace.

There was a big procession coming towards them as Kanji waited his turn among the Princes. And at the head of it was Princess Tara with a garland in her hands. All the Princes pushed forward and took what seemed to them the most attractive poses, whilst their retainers sang their praises. But the Princess looked neither to the right nor to the left. For what she was seeking was a poor boy with a dog by his side.

When Kanji saw her coming near, he made bold to throw him in his new attire, she only kicked it aside and kept on walking. This was a great blow to the boy's pride, so he slipped away quietly and went outside the gate. He found his poor dog waiting for him, so he dismounted from his horse and gathering the poor animal in his arms he fondly hugged him. "If I had

listened to your warning when you tried to remind me
of my father's words, I would not have suffered this
insult today," said he. "But you can be sure my friend,
that I shall not forget it again." Then he sold his horse
and clothes to another fellow, and was soon on the
road again.

Night had fallen by now, and both Kanji and the
dog were resting under a tree, when they heard a company of men coming towards them. Thinking that
they must be some robbers again, Kanji and the dog
quickly climbed the tree and sat there quietly. But as
the company came near, who should they see but the
Princess herself in her palanquin, passing just below
them. At sight of her Kanji trembled with joy, for
indeed she was so beautiful that she put the moon
to shame. The dog seeing his master's plight, and thinking that there was something wrong began to howl.
The Princess heard him, and commanded the palanquin-bearers to stop and find out what was the trouble.
She had set out for the very purpose of finding the dog
and its master, and she wondered if they were hiding in
the tree.

The palanquin-bearers soon found them, and helped
them to descend. And as soon as the Princess saw who
it was, she threw the garland of flowers round Kanji's
neck and proclaimed him her husband. Much to the
astonishment of everybody present.

Kanji asked her why, after spurning him when he
came dressed as a Prince, should she now seek him out
and choose him as her husband. "If you had brought
your faithful companion with you there, then I would

have recognized you. But leaving him somewhere, you came as a cheap imitation of a real Prince, so how do you expect me to know you?" said she. "It was your love towards the poor animal that won my heart, so you must never be without him any more," she added.

Kanji was so overjoyed to hear this that he fell at her feet and thanked her.

They returned to the palace amidst great rejoicings and Kanji sent for his mother and brother to attend the wedding which took place a few days later, with great pomp and splendour. Ever after, Kanji never forgot to keep his dog beside him, for it was due to him that so much happiness had come his way. Also he kept in mind his father's words and never misused the power of the purse, given to him. And was known throughout the land as the most selfless Prince who ever wore a crown.

The Friendly Tree

ONCE upon a time there grew a friendly tree on the banks of the river Kavery. So big was its trunk that it needed more than a dozen children to join hands and encircle it. And its branches spread so wide that a whole flock of sheep could take shelter under them.

In the Spring, when every tree put on its newest garments, and the grass underneath was studded with wild flowers, the friendly tree wore its richest robes, and put forth its red berries, and lovely yellow flowers.

The children came from far and near to eat the berries, and every housewife remembered to take home a bunch of its aromatic flowers, to flavour her cooking. The leaves too were in great favour with the cattle and sheep, and so the poor tree was daily plundered. But being very generous by nature, as often as it was stripped, so often did it put forth everything again.

Many, many, years rolled by thus, while generation after generation of children played around its trunk, grew up to be farmers or shepherds, became old and went to their graves. The friendly tree, remained as friendly as ever.

Then came a time when a great big road was constructed quite near the bank where stood the tree. All day the huge steam roller went forward and backward crushing the stones and earth under its iron wheels. The villagers were informed that the friendly tree was to be cut down to make room for the road. You can imagine their sorrow when they heard of this.

They went in a body to the authorities in charge, to plead for their tree. In vain did they point out what a blessing it would be to the travellers. The authorities refused to listen to them. "Do you know that if we were to curve this road ever so slightly, to save your tree, it would cost us nearly a thousand Rupees?" said they. "Who is to pay this thousand, may I ask?" The poor villagers looked at each other sadly, for a thousand Rupees was a great deal of money. Then one of them ventured timidly, "If somebody were to pay you this amount, would you leave the tree alone?"

"We may consider the proposition," said the authorities, and dismissed them rudely. The poor villagers went home, but none of them could sleep that night. Every man conferred with his wife, and decided to part with some of his cattle, sheep, or land. And every woman insisted on parting with some of her jewellery. To them this tree, where they had played and grown up, was like a great-grand sire, and to have it cut down was unthinkable. So off they went to a nearby town the next day, and smilingly parted with their possessions and handed over the amount to the authorities.

The friendly tree was saved, and as if in gratitude towards all who had sacrificed for its sake, it made a greater effort each year to please young and old alike.

Many years went by, and now the tree was so old that it leaned dangerously over the bank of the river.

The following year brought heavy rains, which destroyed all the crops and left the villagers to face a period of famine. As if this was not enough their beloved tree was uprooted, and went crashing into the water, where it lay clinging to the bank.

There was nothing else to do now but to cut it up as soon as the rains stopped, and sell the wood, which was too good to be used as fuel. Besides, did they not need the money to buy food for their families? So with a heavy heart the villagers set to work.

When they had cut all the branches and were sawing the trunk, they came upon something so hard, that it blunted the teeth of the saw and refused to let it proceed any further.

Much perplexed at this unusual obstruction, the villagers commenced to use their axes. And what should they discover but a very ancient copper pot filled with coins and jewels. Nobody knew how it had got there. Perhaps nearly a century ago when the tree was very young, somebody had hollowed out the trunk and hidden his treasure there. How faithfully the dear tree had guarded the treasure! And how well it had timed its delivery to the starving villagers!

Thus even in death, the friendly tree had proved its loyalty and usefulness. Is it any wonder then that even today if you pass the spot on the banks of the Kavery, you see a stone tablet on which are written just these words. "Here grew the Friendly Tree." And the road makes a wide circle round it.

Princess Petunia Chooses a Husband

THERE was great rejoicing in Flower Land because it was Princess Purple Petunia's birthday, and as she had come of age on that day, her father the King of Petunias wanted her to choose a husband from among the princes who were invited by him.

The Blue Bells had been ringing their bells since dawn, and the Pinks and Pansies were rushing about everywhere helping the Princess with her guests, and arranging the presents they had brought with them.

The bees had roamed the hills to gather their sweetest honey, and the ants their biggest lumps of sugar, whilst the birds, not to be outdone by these, had gone to distant lands to collect rare fruits and seeds. And each and every flower had distilled its best perfume, which they presented to the Princess in tiny green bottles made from their stalks, and corked with mixture of pollen and dew.

The Princess was so happy that she kissed every one of them as she expressed her thanks. Even the ugly toads, who staggered under the weight of their largest stools, and the snakes, scorpions, and centipedes from her garden who had nothing better to give her than their stings and poisons, were treated with the same love and kindness. For the Princess knew that these poor creatures had given her their most precious possessions without which they were likely to lose their lives.

Now Princess Purple had a younger sister called Princess Mauve, who was a very pretty girl, but unfortunately she was so jealous of the popularity of her elder sister, that she sat and moped in her room, instead of coming out and taking part in the rejoicings. But nobody really missed her, because she was too proud to mix with common people, and the common people did not like her.

As the day progressed, more and more princes from Flower Land arrived with their retinue, and it was indeed a wonderful sight to see so many flowers at the same time.

Among those who had come, was the handsome King of the Evening Glories. He had remained a bachelor because till now he had not met a girl who had passed the tests he put to her. And having heard so much about the Princess Purple, his subjects had urged him to try and win her for a bride. And this he promised to do if she passed the test that he was determined to put her to. Accordingly he dressed his clown in his own white clothes and made him ride his white charger, whereas he himself changed into a cactus, and rode on a donkey, behind.

When they arrived at King Petunia's palace, the birthday celebrations were at their height, and Princess Purple was freely mixing with everybody and receiving their felicitations. Princess Mauve, on the other hand, was sitting on a dais, aloof and disdainful, with only her hand-maidens to speak to her. And when the white horse with its rider appeared, followed by the donkey with the cactus, she laughed so much that she almost fell from her chair. And as it was natural, the poor donkey with its charge was ordered to take the remotest corner of the garden. Princess Purple, seeing this insult done to her guest, felt sorry for him, and as soon as she could slip away, she went to the donkey and led him to her own lawn to graze happily. Then turning to the Cactus who was standing under the shade of a tree she said, "Fair sir, I am sorry that you were thus obliged to leave our company, but could you do me the honour of marrying me?"

The Prince was so taken by surprise by the suddenness of this question that for a long while he did not answer. Then at last he said, "Marry YOU? People will think that you had taken leave of your senses! Besides I am full of thorns, and I can only hurt you."

"I would rather be hurt by you than caressed by anybody else. For something tells me that beneath this thorny exterior beats a kind and loving heart. So could you honour me by accepting me as your wife?"

"If you insist I have no choice in the matter," said the King, and hand in hand they returned to the rest of the company.

When the father saw whom she had chosen for her husband he was so shocked he could not even speak. And even her best friends could not understand why she had chosen so ugly and repulsive a creature, when she had such a vast choice. But Princess Purple was firm, and her choice was final, so they could not do anything about it.

The Princess Mauve seeing that the white charger with its rider would go out of her life for ever, entreated her parents to allow her to choose him for a husband, in spite of the fact that she was still under age. And the father who was so much disappointed with his eldest daughter, readily agreed. And a double wedding was celebrated the same day. But no sooner were the couples pronounced man and wife than the cactus changed into the handsome King of the Evening Glories, while the other fellow changed into a clown, who to amuse his newly won spouse commenced to tumble and dance before her. And Princess Mauve burst into tears and said that her sister had planned this deception purposely for her. And the King her father was so angry, he banished his eldest daughter and her husband from his kingdom. In vain did the Princess Purple plead her innocence, her father would not hear her. At last her husband decided to make his confession which he did immediately, and also promised to educate his clown and make him King of half his kingdom. Everybody was pleased to hear this, and both the Princesses left together to commence a new life with their respective husbands. And when their father died, as he had no son, his subjects insisted on choosing his son-in-law the King of the Evening Glories to reign over them, and the people were very happy to have their beloved Princess Purple back as Queen to reign with her husband.

The Man who Grew Roses

ON the green heart of a smiling valley, which echoed with the calls of blackbirds and orioles, there was once a dear little cottage, called "Fairy Dell" where lived the man who grew roses. If you ask me his name or where he came from, I am afraid I couldn't tell you. For when I used to meet him I was a child. And children do not care for names of people or places. What mattered to us then, was the man himself, and what he did. And what he used to do was something wonderful. For there was not a rose in the world he could not grow, nor a garden on earth like the one he had made around his little home. And it was said that even the fairies dwelt there.

No doubt there were other gardens too, in this green and fertile valley, and though these could boast of many a lovely blossom, nowhere would you come across the queen of all flowers—The Rose—, in such beauty and variety.

Each type of rose had a name of course. But it was not "Paul Neron" or the "Black Prince" or the "Bride," such as you find in flower catalogues. Each name was chosen after deep consideration of the rose's merits and special quality.

Thus there was one growing near the gate which was called "Sweet Dreams." And indeed, looking at its fragrant petals, tinged with the hues of twilight, who could doubt its powers to give the sweetest dreams you could ever imagine!

Another, which practically smothered the tiny window of the cottage, was called "Sunshine" and you could almost feel the warmth of its colour on your skin. Whereas from the rose called "Laughter," the silver peals of gaiety rippled on the air, as the pure white blossoms tossed in the breeze.

Yet another called "Happiness" had a charm, I am sure, of driving away all traces of sorrow and trouble from the heart. And there was not an unhappy person who visited this garden, and set his eyes on this marvel in shell-pink and gold, but found his sorrow fade away as the stars fade in the morning light.

There were many others equally beautiful and surprising. And not only as a child, but even today, I believe that Fairyland could not have been more enchanting than this little garden, which was rightly called "Fairy Dell." Nor Heaven itself more fragrant.

Every year when the roses were in bloom, people came from far and near as to a holy shrine, and went away with a gift from the gardener. Given free, but was priceless all the same. For no amount of money could have bought it elsewhere.

And every year when the holidays came, we too went to the same valley, and saw the same old man, who welcomed us to his little garden, showed us his latest creation, and allowed us to kiss any rose we fancied.

But when it came to plucking the roses, he was very particular. And no one was allowed to pick even the most faded of his blooms. He alone would sever it from its companions. And that too after many sweet words

of consolation and apologies, for the pain he was about
to cause.

Never was a bush deprived of more than one blossom
at a time, no matter in what profusion the flowers
grew. He used to say that it was like taking away a
child from its mother. And which mother would wil-
lingly part with her little one even though she has
many others left to her? From all this you will readily
understand how dearly he loved his roses, and how
much he understood about them.

A day came however when we were to receive a rude
shock. It was not the shock of his death. For that too
would have been shocking enough. But the greater
shock of the disappearance of the gardener himself.
And his replacement by a rude young man, who wore
spectacles.

We had gone as usual to meet our friend during our
Divali holidays, and play in his lovely little garden.
But instead of the smiling old gardener, with a battered
straw hat, who came running to open the gate for us,
saying, "Come in, Come in. And how are you my little
ones?" Then turning to my cousin and making the
same old remark, "Dear me! How you have grown!
You will be taller than the tallest of my roses." Here was
a tall muscular man who frowned at us. And shooed us
away saying, "Get yourself gone! And don't dare to
come here again."

My friend Nadir, who was a little bolder than the
rest of us, stood his ground saying, "We haven't come
to see YOU, MISTER.... We have come to see the old
gardener who stays here, and who is our friend."

"He is your friend indeed! Is he?" asked the rude man. "Then go and look for him elsewhere. For he no longer stays here."

"Can we play in the garden as we used to?" asked my cousin, not being happy at the idea of going away without seeing our old friend.

"Play in this garden!" screamed the young man. "Why, you must be mad to think of such a thing! A couple of brats like you would ruin this garden in no time! Get yourself gone, and make haste about it, or I will bring a stick and beat you with it," said the nasty fellow.

We were so shocked at this that we could not reply, and stood looking at the poor roses who were half dead and drooping. And feeling as miserable as ourselves.

Then Nadir whispered into my ear. "I know what has happened to the old man. He has been locked up in the cottage, and this other one, who is a pirate, has taken away the garden from him. For don't you see that red handkerchief round the head?"

"A pirate!" I said in surpise. "You mean a brigand?"

"I mean one of those nasty chaps who tie kerchiefs round their heads, and who have a band of robbers under them."

"All right! All right! Shut up," said my cousin, who was getting more and more nervous. "Let's not stand here and argue. For at any moment he will call his robbers who will carry us away to a cave or dungeon. Let's run and call the police."

So off we ran helter skelter, shouting "Police!

Police!" but no policeman answered us.

It was not till we had gone a long way that we met a postman going his rounds. We told our story to him as soon as we could recover our breath. But the postman only laughed and laughed. "You children don't seem to know the story," said he. "And if I stop here to tell it to you I will be very late with my letters. So you go to that little house there, and the dear old lady who lives in it will be glad to have you, and to tell you every thing."

We did not wait to be told twice, but ran off to the house he had pointed out, and knocked at the gate. And just as the postman had said, out came a small old lady with silver grey hair tied in a bun behind her head. She smiled so sweetly that we forgot our troubles.

"Now let me see," said she, squinting at us and coming nearer with the help of a stick. "Are you children? Or are you fairies?"

"We are children," we said in a chorus. We were very pleased that she had mistaken us for fairies, for that meant two things. Either we looked like fairies, which was very flattering, or that fairies were in the habit of visiting this place, which was quite exciting.

The old lady opened the gate and we trooped in after her. She gave us a mat to sit on the verandah, while she went inside and brought us some strawberries, which she said she had grown in her garden. And we were so hungry after our long run, that very soon we had finished all of them. And we even forgot why we had come.

"Do fairies come here?" I asked timidly.

"Oh yes, my child," said the old lady. "Not only do they come here, but they live here all the time."

"Where?" we asked together.

"Oh, all over the place," said she looking everywhere. "Ever since that nasty young man took over 'Fairy Dell,' they fled from there and are living in my garden."

"Oh," said I. "Now I remember. We came here just to ask you about 'Fairy Dell.' Where is the old man who used to look after it? The postman said you would tell us."

Hearing this the old lady became very grave. "It is a sad story my pets, and I would not like to trouble your little heads about it. But since you wish to know, I can tell you this much. 'Fairy Dell' belonged to an old gentleman who rarely visited the cottage. But a few months ago he died and left all he owned to a nephew. This young man lost no time in coming down here, and when he saw the lovely roses, he plucked and carried away a cartload of them. The old gardener was in tears to see his beloved flowers treated so heartlessly. But what could he do? All his protests were in vain. As if this was not enough, a few days afterwards, he was served with a notice to leave the place. And the rude young man you speak about, was put instead. He is supposed to be very clever and has taken a degree in rose culture. But he hasn't been able to produce a single bloom on his own, which would be worth mentioning."

We were relieved to hear this in one way, because that meant that our dear old friend was not locked up in the cottage, as Nadir had feared. And there was a chance of our seeing him one day.

"Served him right!" said my cousin, after listening to the story. "I hope all the thorns on the rose bushes will prick him each time he goes near them."

"But what happened to the poor old gardener?" I asked. "My friend here imagined that this new fellow had locked him up in the cottage."

The old lady smiled at hearing this. "Oh no," said she. "The poor fellow had to leave the place. And he went away with a broken heart. Many of us offered to keep him, but he said that it was no use staying in the place where his children—the roses—,were being ill-treated. So one night he bade the dear roses goodbye, with many a tear shed over their petals, and went his way. Nobody knows where he has gone. And that very night, the fairies who lived in the rose bushes also fled. And the poor roses are dying slowly, as you have noticed. For it is not manure, water, and the weather alone, that can make them grow, but the love and tender care of a gardener, like the old man."

Tears were running down our cheeks when the old lady finished her story, and we had to make a great effort to control ourselves. The old lady too wiped her eyes. For it was not the loss of a dear friend alone, which was hurting all of us. But the loss of so much beauty, which we would never see again.

"When I grow up," said my cousin, "I too will be a gardener. And will grow roses like the old man."

"That's a good idea my little one," said the lady. "I wish you the best of luck. If I am alive, I shall come and have a look at them."

We left "Happy Cottage" as this place was called, after this. And promised to return there during our next holidays.

We never went near "Fairy Dell" after this. But we often chased butterflies at "Happy Cottage" making-believe that they were fairies. We never saw a real fairy either, though the old lady always told us that she was just round the corner.

Each time we went to the same valley, we did so in the hope of seeing our dear friend the gardener. But he never returned to the old place. And his memory shall always remain in our hearts as the one man who knew how to grow roses, and to adore them.

The Ways of the Great

ONCE upon a time, in the town of Bhishapur, their lived a powerful man who was not only a dispenser of justice, but the head of all the people of the place. Everybody loved and feared him at the same time. And the very mention of the word "Kajee" was enough to strike terror in the boldest heart. "Kajee" of course means the head priest, but he is also chief justice and many other things too.

Now the Kajee had a servant called Kadar who worshipped his master. But Kadar had one defect. In his eagerness to serve his master diligently, he was often thoughtlessly hasty and brusque. So it happened that when the Kajee was engaged in some important work, his servant would burst into the room with some trivial news, such as Amina his neighbour's cow, had given birth to a calf, or Kasim's son had spilled ink on his brother's shirt.

At last the Kajee was very tired of this interference and sent for Kadar and said, "Now look here. If you ever burst into my room again and bother me with unimportant things, I shall dismiss you on the spot. I have had enough of your nonsense. If you cannot learn to control yourself, I shall be much happier without your services. So remember this, and hammer it into your head, that no matter what happens, or however important the news may seem to you, you have never to rush into my presence and disturb me with it. If you MUST

He noticed that a big spark from the Hooka of one of the guests had set alight his master's turban.

tell me something, think twice before you do so. Learn to act with calm and control. Or by my beard, I swear I shall kick you out of my house!"

Poor Kadar was so upset on hearing this, that he decided to hold his tongue hereafter. And to let the other servants carry the news to the master.

Many days passed smoothly after this. Then came the great day of the Conference. Kadar was posted at the door to admit the learned men who came there. And as he was performing his duty, to his utter surprise, he noticed that a big spark from the Hooka (Hubble-Bubble) of one of the guests had set alight his master's turban. His first impulse was to rush in and shout a warning to his master. But he remembered the latter's threat and checked himself. Then with both hands raised in supplication he meekly approached the high chair on which his master was seated, and began thus "Ka-Jee-Jee. Your---Tur--ba--n" but before he could go any further there was a scream from his master; for by now, not only the turban of the Kajee but also his scalp was singed.

Everybody rushed to help the great man, and when the confusion had become simmered down, the Kajee called his servant to him and shouted "You fool! What did you mean by standing there lisping whilst my head was getting burnt! Out of my presence before I beat you till your teeth fall out. You are worse than an ass...."

Poor Kadar did not know where to look and what to say. He began weeping like a child, and to tremble all over. "Strange are the ways of the great," he cried.

"When I spoke hastily, my master accused me of being impatient, and now when I behave with calm, I am told that I am a fool. It is indeed very difficult to serve anybody faithfully nowadays." So saying he was about to leave but the Kajee's wife who had seen and heard everything from behind her Purdah or veil, fell at her husband's feet and begged for mercy for the poor man. And much against his will, the Kajee was obliged to take him back.